CHADO
THE JAPANESE WAY OF TEA

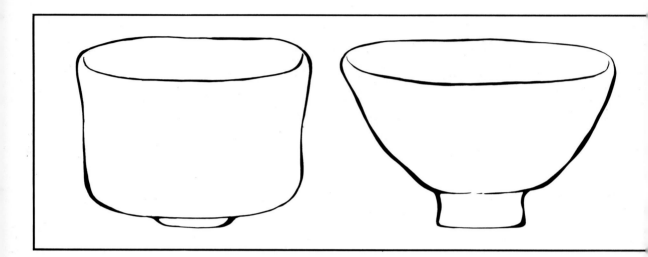

CHADO

THE JAPANESE WAY OF TEA

by Soshitsu Sen

Grand Master XV, Urasenke School of Tea

Weatherhill / Tankosha   *New York • Tokyo • Kyoto*

This book has been adapted for Western readers from two books in Japanese by the same author, both published by Tankosha in 1977: *Asu e no chado nyumon* (Introduction to Tea for Tomorrow) and *Chaji* (The Tea Gathering). Translated and edited by Masuo Yamaguchi, James T. Conte, Nancy Yamada, Takeya Yamasaki, Charles C. Santon, and Akiko Mori.

First edition, 1979
Fourth printing, 1998

Jointly published by Weatherhill, Inc., of New York and Tokyo, with editorial offices at 568 Broadway, Suite 705, New York, N.Y. 10012, and Tankosha, of Kyoto. Copyright © 1979 by Soshitsu Sen; all rights reserved. Printed in Hong Kong.

Library of Congress Cataloging in Publication Data: Sen, Sōshitsu, 1923– / Chadō: the Japanese way of tea. / Adapted from Asu e no chadō nyūmon and the author's Chaji. / Includes index. / 1. Japanese tea ceremony. / I. Yamaguchi, Masuo. / II. Sen, Soshitsu, 1923– Chaji. / III. Asu e no chadō nyūmon. / IV. Title. / GT 2910.S4335 / 1979 / 394.1'2 / 78–26503 / ISBN 0-8348-1518-4

CONTENTS

PREFACE

JAPAN, ITS BIRTH HIDDEN in the mists of legend and myth, presents a special problem to those people who wish to comprehend and appreciate a culture that is different from their own. However, these mists, like those that often shroud the mountains that surround the old capital of Kyoto, are slowly vanishing with the dawn of Japan's entry into the world community. Daily there are announcements of the unlocking of some part of Japanese culture. Whether it be reported as a new technological development or as a fresh insight into the way that the Japanese think, all the announcements would lead one to believe that Japan is changing.

Since Commodore Perry's ships anchored in Uraga Bay in 1853, Japanese culture has gradually become more and more westernized, or at least that is the way it seems. I say "seems" because, looking closely and comparing the way Western practices and technology have been assimilated into the daily life of a typical Japanese, one cannot help but feel there is a slight difference. This difference is due to the firm foundation of the Japanese culture.

In terms of global history, Japan has only recently joined the mainstream of world events. Never until World War II had Japan been subjected to an invasion or occupation, except that of ideas. Of course, there have been enormous internal conflicts, but they have contributed to the tempering of the national character. Contained on a long and narrow string of islands, Japanese culture developed along a special path.

From the standpoint of their culture, the Japanese have a unique point of view that makes for a certain degree of immunity to influence from outside sources. Similar to the course of their adoption of large sections of Chinese culture some 1,300 years ago, the Japanese today are still caught in the initial frenzy of imitation. Once the dust settles, what will be left will undoubtedly be that which would be useful in almost any culture.

People of the West are now showing an interest in Oriental traditions in general and those of Japan in particular. Hopefully this interest in traditions will mature into an understanding of Japanese culture once its basis is understood. Going beyond the novelty of the strange and exotic and seeking out these most basic components of Japanese culture, one will be better able to assimilate what has been found in daily life.

Chanoyu, popularly known as the Japanese tea ceremony, may at first glance seem to be very formalized and stereotyped, but it has a long history and has become deeply rooted in the daily life of the Japanese. Although there are many types of tea in Japan, these can be divided into three general categories: *bancha* (coarse leaf tea), *sencha* (medium-quality green tea), and *matcha* (powdered green tea). In addition, each of these has various grades within it. When serving coarse or medium-quality green tea, no special formalities are observed. If, however, powdered green tea is served, both the host and the guest generally follow certain rules of etiquette.

After the guest has finished some sweets, he is offered a bowl of matcha, the powdered tea having been whipped with hot water. The guest responds to this expression of hospitality by complimenting the host on the taste and appearance of the sweets and the beauty of the serving dish, and then praising the tea and the tea bowl. When, where, and by whom the bowl was made are important topics of conversation between host and guest. If the guest is served in a Japanese-style room, the hanging scroll and flowers in the tokonoma are also commented upon. The origin and meaning of the scroll are usually discussed in detail. This etiquette may sound somewhat exaggerated, but even in the Western world a guest will express his thanks if he is given a cup of tea by his host. In Japan, however, a simple remark of gratitude is not considered adequate when a bowl of powdered green tea is served. Since the host has taken great pains to prepare the tea and select the sweets, an equally appropriate response is expected from the guest. All of this—the concept of etiquette based upon the mutual contribution of the host and guest to the mood of their meeting—is a part of everyday life in Japan and not something to be observed just at a formal tea gathering.

I believe that Chado, the Japanese way of tea, is one of the best ways that one can come to understand the foundations of Japanese culture. To follow the way of tea is not easy, but, convinced that one best understands something through experiencing it, I would therefore like to introduce you to the tradition and practice of Chado. With this glimpse into the way of tea, you will have an opportunity to see how the culture of Japan has been influenced by it. But, even more than this, you will find that the principles of Chado know no boundaries and can be applied anywhere in the world.

First I will discuss the meaning and the history and development of Chado in Japan. Next follows an introduction to the tea setting, utensils, and cuisine. Finally I will describe a standard tea gathering in terms of setting, utensils, cuisine, and step-by-step procedures, following a tea gathering from the time the guest receives an invitation, through the partaking of the tea, up to the final farewell of the host as the guests return home through the garden. For those throughout the world who wish to practice and enjoy tea gatherings, this example should be kept in mind, even if adaptations have to be made to meet the exigencies of time and place.

S. S.

1

INTRODUCTION

THE SPIRIT OF TEA Without concern for cultural or religious differences, Chado speaks directly to the humanity of people. Without concern for national origins, the spirit of tea enriches all those people who practice it. What does "spirit" mean? Perhaps a few stories and thoughts might best convey the answer.

First a story from the time of Buddha. A man was walking deep in the mountains, looking for a place where he could discipline himself toward understanding his spirit. While searching, he chanced to meet one of Buddha's disciples. "Sir, from where do you come?" he asked. The disciple answered, "I've come from my place of practice." Thinking that this was the place for which he had been searching, he asked the disciple, "Please, sir, I am looking for that same place. Please take me there." The disciple answered, "The place of practice lies in the pure and honest spirit." Startled, the man realized that a place of practice and discipline is not seen only with the eyes.

Another story is of a Chinese poet who was preparing for an official assignment in a distant province. He decided to seek out a teacher because soon he was to lead many people and he wished to govern them well. He visited a famous Zen monk to ask for advice. The monk, who had no temple, always sat in meditation at the top of a tree. Standing at the foot of the tree, the poet asked what the ideal spirit is, and what he should do now that he must govern. The priest did not move. Unsure of what to do, the poet looked up at the monk from below and said, "If you doze off sitting up there, you'll fall and hurt yourself, won't you?" Hearing this, the monk called back, "What are you saying? Your feet aren't even touching the ground, are they?" The poet was so surprised by the monk's words that he looked afresh at his own feet, and he realized that they were not on the ground. With that, he bowed and begged to be allowed to hear the monk's teachings. The monk said, "That's easy. A leader does good for the common people; he does not commit any evil acts." The monk then said that this is all of the Buddha's teachings, and if only these things are done, the poet-turned-governor would govern his province well. The poet replied that anyone could do good and not do evil. The monk stormed back, "If that is so then I will become your student and you will be my teacher."

Someone once asked the great sixteenth-century tea master Sen Rikyu, "What is tea?" Rikyu answered him, "Tea is not difficult. Suggest coolness in summer and warmth in winter. Set the charcoal so that the water will boil. The flowers should be arranged as if they were still in the field." To that the man said, "Anyone can do that." Rikyu, too, replied, "If that is so, then I will become your student and you will be my teacher."

Rikyu codified the rules of etiquette for drinking a bowl of tea. His reason for this was that if people did not know these rules, they would be unsure as to the best movements of the body and thus would not be able to perform well. In the words of Rikyu, "Shelter is enough if it protects from the rain, and food is sufficient if it satisfies hunger. With your own hands, bring wood and water, boil the water, make tea, offer it at the altar, share it with others, and drink it yourself. One also arranges flowers and burns incense. These actions are taken together for the purpose of studying the deeds of Buddha." This, too, seems a simple enough thing when first heard. But just how easy is it? Please try yourselves to boil water, using cold water and charcoal. Then make tea, offer it at your altar, share it with others, and then drink it yourself. Though it may sound easy, you will find it a difficult thing to do.

Another meaning of spirit can be seen in a simple greeting. The Japanese are fond of *aisatsu* (greetings). *Ai* means "friendship," and *satsu* means "to draw forth each other's good qualities through acquaintance." Exchanging bows is true aisatsu only when it is felt that at that instant something good is brought out from both parties. Recently, however, the meaning of greeting has deteriorated. Human relationships now are based on the self alone, which leaves no space for reaching out and seeking the good in others. When we lose our warm feelings for others, the meaning vanishes, even though the form still exists.

Today's world is filled with knowledge. Knowledge and wisdom, I think, have to be considered on different levels. In our highly developed world, knowledge can usually be easily obtained if one so desires and makes the effort. It is wisdom, however, that enables one to apply acquired knowledge and give it value. Knowledge is obtained by reading books and newspapers, watching television, hearing lectures, and so on. But knowledge in itself is empty. To be of value, it must be put into practice and continuously applied in response to ever-changing circumstances. This, then, is wisdom. It is the best application of knowledge.

In the practice of tea, a sanctuary is created where one can take solace in the tranquility of the spirit. The utensils are carefully selected, and, like the tearoom and garden path, they are cleaned; the writing of a man of virtue is hung in the tokonoma and flowers picked that very morning are placed beneath it. The light is natural, but dim and diffused, casting no shadow, and the kettle simmers over the glowing charcoal embers. The setting thus created is conducive to reflection and introspection. Making tea for oneself in such a setting is sublime. Here man, nature, and the spirit are brought together through the preparation and drinking of tea. Sitting alone, drinking tea is a microcosm complete in every way.

Receiving guests within the microcosm of the tea setting necessitates the implementation of particular measures to maintain this tranquility. Sen Rikyu believed that certain guidelines were necessary for the host and guest during a tea gathering. But they are principles that can be followed whether in the tearoom or the everyday world. The principles of tea Rikyu set forth are harmony, respect, purity, and tranquility. Harmony is the oneness of host and guest with the flowing rhythms of nature. The harmonious atmosphere of a tea gathering depends upon the union of host and guest—a union that must be absolutely sincere and truthful. When the guests enter the microcosm of the tea setting, they should be in harmony with it, just as is the host. Respect is the sincerity of heart that allows one to have an open relationship with the other participants, humbly recognizing their dignity. To discipline oneself to be humble enables one to see the world as it truly is. Purity is removing the dust of the world from one's heart and mind. Cleaning in preparation for a tea gathering, the host also establishes order within himself. As he sees to the details of the teahouse and the garden path, he is no less attending to his own consciousness and to the state of mind with which he will serve his guests. Tranquility comes with the constant practice of harmony, respect, and purity in everyday life. In this state of mind, having found peace within oneself, a bowl of tea can truly be shared with another.

The spirit of tea is the search to do good and not to do evil. It is a greeting that reaches out and seeks the good in others. It is the wisdom that comes from applying knowledge each moment in response to circumstance. It is the host inviting a guest to share peace in a bowl of tea.

THE STUDY OF TEA   A great part of the beauty of a tea gathering is in the movements of the participants. The student of tea should remember that, above all, the key to those movements lies in the spirit and dedication of the individual; if one is not completely committed to what one is doing, the tea gathering will lose its meaning, no matter how accomplished one may be at carrying out the proper movements.

A tea gathering is a meeting of host and guest regulated to a certain extent by procedure and pace. Awaiting the host's entrance into the tearoom, the guests sit quietly, absorbing the tranquil atmosphere created by the room and the tea utensils that have been chosen for the occasion. When the host appears and begins to make tea, his movements are meant to maintain that tranquility. At times his actions will be abrupt, at others, slow and measured. Certain movements of his may seem tense, others smooth and methodic. But it is these very differences in pace and concentration that create the beauty and texture of a tea gathering. And each reflects the host's concentration, dedication, and spirit. One may memorize all the movements perfectly, but if these are not carried out with the proper spirit, the tranquility of the gathering will be lost. At the same time, although a host may be rather unskilled in the movements, if he proceeds with his whole being, the guests will sense this, and the tea he makes will reflect his spirit. Thus it is the combination of skill and spirit that creates the true meaning of the way of tea.

The process of learning to make tea properly is a slow, exacting one. The teacher's goal is to inculcate in the student the correct psychological attitude needed when, for example, purifying the tea scoop or serving the tea to the guest. What is necessary is complete concentration, no matter what aspect of the procedure one is carrying out. As the student gradually understands this, it is an attitude that will become a part of his everyday life, present in everything be does.

THE HISTORY OF TEA   Tea has for so long been a common drink around the world that people usually take its history for granted. It is known that as early as 2780 B.C. a Chinese, investigating the properties of various herbs, roots, and plants, found that a brew made from tea leaves was a refreshing drink that relieved fatigue. During the T'ang dynasty (618–907) Lu Yu wrote his treatise *Ch'a Ching,* a detailed study of tea. His book was a mine of historical, botanical, and medical information pertaining to tea, and included information on how to cultivate, brew, serve, and drink it. The method of preparing tea that Lu Yu discussed is in some ways similar to that which is used in outdoor tea gatherings today. When the tea leaves were picked, they were stacked, shaped, and pressed into a mold, and then dried, forming a hard, bricklike mass. To brew this, the brick was broiled and separated over a fire, crushed in a mortar, and then mixed with hot water in a kettle. After the leaves had settled in the kettle, the infused water was drunk.

Tea was probably first imported to Japan during the regency of Prince Shotoku (572–622). During that time, Japan was going through one of its three great periods of cultural importation from China. One of the most important things being adopted then by the Japanese was Buddhism, and many Japanese priests went to China to study this new religion. It was these men who brought tea back to their homeland. But the cultivation of tea did not catch on very readily in Japan. In fact, it was not until 806 that the priest Kukai (774–835) introduced into Japan the method of brewing tea from leaves. During the reign of Emperor Saga (786–842), court nobles used tea for medicinal purposes, but after the tenth century even this practice died out, and tea drinking disappeared from Japan.

In the late twelfth century the priest Eisai (1141–1215) went to study Zen Buddhism in China. While on the mainland, he realized that tea was an indispensable part of Zen temple life. When he returned to Japan in 1191, he brought with him some seeds and attempted to use tea as a tool for propagating Zen in Japan. Successful in growing tea in the area of the present Fukuoka Prefecture, Eisai convinced the priest Myoe (1173–1232) to plant seeds at the Kozan-ji temple in Kyoto, where the plants eventually flourished. Eisai wrote a book entitled *Kissa Yojoki* (Preservation of Health Through Drinking Tea) in which he extolled the medicinal virtues of tea, saying it added to the drinker's health and longevity. He even told the shogun Minamoto Sanetomo (1192–1219) that tea was effective in alleviating hangovers. Tea was at this time viewed as a medicine. Tea cultivation spread from Kozan-ji to Uji, south of Kyoto. As the availability of tea increased, more and more court nobles and families of high rank began to drink it, primarily as a refreshment by this time.

By the fourteenth century, tea drinking had spread from the upper classes to the samurai, Buddhist clergy, and even some commoners. At this time, tea gatherings became quite popular among the samurai class. These gatherings centered around a contest called *tocha* in which stakes were wagered and participants vied with one another to distinguish different teas by taste.

At the same time, tea drinking was developing into a solemn ceremony at Buddhist temples. In the appointed room, a picture of Shakyamuni might be hung in the tokonoma along with a *kakemono* (hanging scroll) from China. Flowers would be arranged in a Chinese vase and incense burned in a brazier that had also been imported from China. This fascination with things made in China spread to the samurai, who began to employ articles imported from China to decorate the rooms used for playing tocha.

Gradually, tea drinking was becoming a part of Japanese life. By 1400 tea was being sold on the streets to commoners. But the method of preparing and drinking tea was becoming more and more systematized. The shogun Ashikaga Yoshimasa (1435–90) retained Noami (1397–1471) and his grandson Soami (1472–1523); under these two men *shoin cha* (a tea gathering held in a reception room and employing Chinese utensils) became more formalized and fashionable. It was during this period that the *daisu* (the Chinese stand used for holding tea utensils) was introduced into shoin cha. As this kind of tea gathering became more popular with the upper classes, the reception rooms in which it was held became more lavish and gorgeously appointed.

As a reaction to this, Murata Shuko (1422–1502) devised a new style of tea gathering to be held in a small room with a limited number of guests. This was called *soan cha,* or grass-hut tea. Shuko had first studied the style of shoin cha and later became a disciple of the Zen Buddhist priest Ikkyu (1394–1481). It was the austerity and simplicity of the latter that led him to serve tea in a small tearoom of only four-and-one-half tatami (nine feet square). In this confined, austere room, its tokonoma ornamented with only a single hanging scroll, he pursued the beauty of the way of tea, using simple, imperfect Japanese utensils as well as more sophisticated Japanese and Chinese utensils. Gradually the popularity of the lavish shoin cha gave way to that of the simple soan cha. Perhaps this was caused by the uncertainty and strife of the Onin Civil War (1467–77); surrounded by death and suffering, people sought beauty and consonance, and the intimate, austere setting of soan cha meant that all who attended must be in harmony with one another.

The Onin Civil War left the samurai class as a whole in straitened circumstances. But merchants thrived as a result of the civil strife and accumulated vast fortunes. One such man was Takeno Jo-o (1504–55), who lived in Sakai, a port city located near present-day Osaka. Jo-o studied tea under Sochin, a disciple of Shuko, and became one of the leading tea masters of his day. Like many other merchants who became interested in tea, he would hold large, lavish tea gatherings in order to display his collection of expensive tea utensils and art objects to his friends and rivals. Merchants were not the only people infected with this exhibitionism; Oda Nobunaga (1534–81), one of the three great unifiers of Japan, reportedly gave a huge tea gathering so that he could flaunt the collection of precious tea utensils and art objects he had assembled.

Sen Rikyu (or Soeki, 1522–91) succeeded Takeno Jo-o as the acknowledged tea master of his day. With Rikyu's guidance, soan cha became known as *wabi cha,* or the tea of quiet taste. Under Nobunaga, peace was gradually restored in Japan. Many of the feudal lords followed Nobunaga's example and took up the practice of tea. Nobunaga was succeeded by Toyotomi Hideyoshi (1536–98). Although Hideyoshi had studied the simple and austere wabi cha under Rikyu, he preferred the lavishness and glitter that characterized the arts of Momoyama-period Japan (1568–1603). At his direction, a tearoom was built with gold foil covering its walls and appointed with a gold daisu, a gold *furo* (portable brazier), and a gold *natsume* (jujube-shaped tea container). Clearly, the spirit of Hideyoshi's tea gatherings was at odds with that of wabi cha, which emphasized simplicity and the curbing of the host's exhibitionist tendencies. In 1587, at Kitano Temman-gu shrine near Kyoto, Hideyoshi held a grand tea gathering. Commanding all those who practiced tea to appear with their own utensils, he himself made a showy display of his own magnificent collection.

Like Nobunaga, Hideyoshi chose to retain Rikyu as his tea master. But the differences between Hideyoshi and Rikyu in their approaches to and philosophies of the way of tea did not bode well for the tea master. Eventually Rikyu angered Hideyoshi and was ordered to commit suicide. The sixty-nine-year-old Rikyu, who had brought wabi cha to the peak of refinement, carried out this order at his home in Sakai in 1591.

Furuta Oribe (1543–1615) succeeded Rikyu as Hideyoshi's tea master. After Tokugawa Ieyasu (1542–1616) completed the unification of Japan in 1630, Oribe eventually became tea master for the second Tokugawa shogun, Hidetada (1579–1632). But, accused of disloyalty to the Tokugawa, he was forced to commit suicide.

Before his death, Oribe had inaugurated the teaching of *daimyo cha,* or tea for the To-kugawa feudal lords, a responsibility inherited by Kobori Enshu (1579–1647). The responsibility for continuing the wabi cha of Sen Rikyu was meanwhile passed down to Rikyu's grandson Sen Sotan (1578–1658). Enshu, who was also an expert garden designer and calligrapher, became the tea master for the third Tokugawa shogun, Iemitsu (1604–58). Under Enshu's supervision and patronage the so-called Seven Enshu Kilns, which produced tea utensils, flourished.

Sen Sotan was twice invited to become the shogun's tea master and twice refused; perhaps he feared that he might share the same fate as his grandfather, who had also been the recipient of favors from men of power. Although Sotan spent his time teaching the wabi-cha style of tea to townspeople, three of his sons taught it to various feudal lords. In this way, the Sen family actively propagated wabi cha among tradesmen and samurai alike. When Sotan retired, he divided his property between three of his sons, each of whom established a school of tea: the Urasenke school, the Omote-Senke school, and the Mushanokoji-Senke school, all of which have continued in existence until today.

Katagiri Sekishu (1605–73) became the tea master for the fourth Tokugawa shogun, Ietsuna (1641–80). Sekishu firmly believed that tea should reflect the tightly structured social system that the Tokugawa rulers were creating. His teachings stood in opposition to the wabi cha of Sen Rikyu, for Sekishu maintained that social distinctions among guests at a tea gathering should be recognized and upheld. Almost all of the feudal lords of that day studied under Sekishu, and the succeeding shoguns also became patrons of the Sekishu school. Many feudal lords also retained resident tea masters in their fiefs, paying them annual stipends. In the course of the Tokugawa period (1603–1868), Matsudaira Fumai (1751–1818), whose fief was on the Japan Sea coast, became the feudal lord who was most involved in the practice of tea. Fumai amassed a great collection of tea utensils, which he had catalogued in detail.

Beginning in the 1850s, the West gradually forced Japan to end its almost 250 years of self-imposed seclusion and open the country to the rest of the world. This process culminated in 1868 with the Meiji Restoration, which destroyed the power of the Tokugawa family and ended the feudal system, returning Japan to imperial rule. As a result of deep-seated changes that Japan underwent thereafter as it struggled to become a modern nation-state, the way of tea entered a new era.

First of all, almost all of the tea masters who had been serving the old government and the various feudal lords lost their positions and their stipends, forcing many of them to look for new livelihoods. Then the new government attempted to discredit the way of tea because of the close connections it had with the old feudal system. But the then Grand Tea Master of the Urasenke school, Gengensai (1810–77), came to the defense of the way of tea, saying that the true spirit of the way of tea made no distinction between rich and poor, high and low. The way of tea, Gengensai went on, taught people to be thrifty and frugal, and to obey rules and regulations—characteristics that the new government counted as virtues. As a result of his urgings, the way of tea was allowed to continue and fend for itself. The situation, however, remained difficult. In addition to the tea masters losing their stipends, many of the feudal lords were placed in financial straits and forced to sell their collections of tea utensils.

By the late nineteenth century, the way of tea was able to regain its footing, but this time upon a different foundation. While previously it has been a pastime of the wealthy and privileged, it now had a much more popular basis. People such as Don-o Masuda (1847–1938), a prominent businessman, became interested in the way of tea and began collecting many of the tea utensils and decorations that had been placed on the market. Following his example, many other businessmen in the Taisho (1912–26) and Showa (1926–present) eras also took up the practice of tea. Some of the most prominent of these people came together to form the famous Daishi-kai, an association for the way of tea. The three Senke schools flourished as a result of this, for they had long directed their energies toward bringing the way of tea to the common man. Other schools such as Sekishu, which had been associated with the hereditary privileged classes, eventually disappeared as their bases of support shrank and then practically disappeared.

An even more important change was the study of the way of tea by women in Japan. Although historically a pastime for men only, following the Sino-Japanese War (1894–95), women also began to participate in tea gatherings. This was primarily through the endeavors of Ennosai, the thirteenth-generation Grand Tea Master of Urasenke, who taught war widows and other women, many of whom obtained instructor's diplomas. During the Taisho era, instruction in the way of tea spread to girls' higher schools as well as to Buddhist convents. With the inclusion of women in the way of tea, the influence of the Senke schools spread throughout Japan.

Gradually the way of tea also became known and practiced in the West. In 1906 Tenshin (or Kakuzo) Okakura published *The Book of Tea* in the United States. In this he explained the metaphysical aspects of tea to his Western audience. But it was not until after World War II that a real interest developed in the West. I myself have traveled abroad widely promoting the study of tea, as have many members of Urasenke, and our school is rapidly establishing branches in major cities around the world. Through these activities we have found that many foreigners are eager to study the way of tea.

2

STRUCTURES AND GARDEN

INTRODUCTION   The garden and structures that are the setting for a tea gathering display a simplicity and naturalness that belie the thought and craftsmanship that go into their construction. Heavily influenced by Zen aesthetics, the purpose of the tea setting is to strip the individual of his worldly cares and transpose him into an environment where, through participation in a tea gathering, he can cleanse his thoughts of the mundane and unimportant, undergoing an experience that is almost spiritual in nature. The mood is one of quietude and peace, and the setting helps to evoke this in all who participate.

The guests approach the tea setting through the main gate, around which water has been sprinkled by the host to indicate that the preparations for the tea gathering are completed and the guests are invited to enter. Going into the *genkan* (entryway), they remove their *zori* (thonged sandals) and go into the *yoritsuki* (changing room), where they deposit their outer wraps and parcels. In the *machiai* (waiting room) they admire the decorations and sip hot water before proceeding to the *koshikake machiai* (sheltered waiting arbor) where they sit and admire the *roji* (garden path). It is here that the host finally comes to greet them, silently inviting them into the tearoom. The guests then proceed through the garden, passing through a small gate, and wash their hands and rinse their mouths at the *tsukubai* (stone water basin), after which they enter the tearoom through the *nijiriguchi* (guest entrance). It is here that the actual tea gathering takes place.

THE GATE   The host has sprinkled water around the gate to inform the guests that preparations for the tea gathering have been completed and they are now invited to enter. Shown here is the famous Kabuto-mon (Helmet Gate) leading into the Urasenke complex in Kyoto.

WAITING ROOM The guests gather in the waiting room before proceeding to the sheltered ▷
waiting arbor. Here they view the decorations in the tokonoma and sip hot water.

THE ENTRYWAY Here guests remove
their thonged sandals before stepping up into the
hallway.

CHANGING ROOM The guests remove
their outer wraps in here and put on fresh, white
tabi (Japanese split-toed socks). Everything but the
articles that they will actually need for the tea
gathering is left in the changing room.

STONE WATER BASIN Before entering the teahouse, the guests stop to wash their hands ▷
and rinse out their mouths at the stone water basin.

GARDEN The garden consists of a moss-covered stone path surrounded by shrubbery and pine trees. The mood varies as the shifting light filters through the branches. The steppingstones have been dampened to create a cooling, refreshing atmosphere.

SHELTERED WAITING ARBOR The guests move from the waiting room to the sheltered waiting arbor, where they sit on cushions that are provided for them. They stay here until the host comes and silently bows, bidding them to enter the teahouse.

(facing page) TEAHOUSE   This teahouse has a thatched roof, and walls of mud and wattle. The small, sliding wooden door is the guest entrance. The size of the entrance necessitates that the guest crouch and enter on his hands and knees, an action symbolizing his humility. A pair of straw sandals rests against the wall.

(left) TEAROOM   It is here that the actual serving of tea takes place.

(below, left) TOKONOMA   The tokonoma of the tearoom, decorated with a hanging scroll and flowers.

(below, right) PREPARATION ROOM   The preparation room *(mizuya)* is next to the tearoom. Only the host and his assistants use this area. It is here that the various tea utensils are stored and the preparations for each stage of the tea gathering are done. Everything is organized for the greatest efficiency.

(overleaf) PLAN OF TEA STRUCTURES AND GARDEN   The diagram shows the plan ▷ for a typical tea garden and structures.

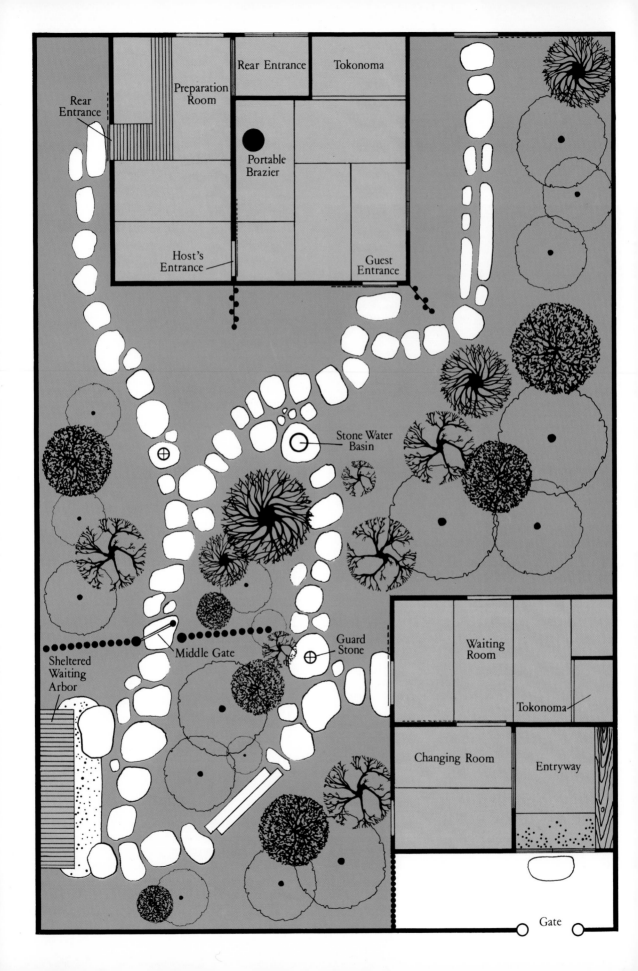

Rear
Entrance

Preparation
Room

Rear Entrance

Tokonoma

Portable
Brazier

Host's
Entrance

Guest
Entrance

Stone Water
Basin

Sheltered
Waiting
Arbor

Middle Gate

Guard Stone

Waiting
Room

Tokonoma

Changing Room

Entryway

Gate

3

UTENSILS AND DECORATIONS

INTRODUCTION The first things that strike a guest when entering a tearoom through the guest entrance are the fragrance of the incense and the beautiful manner in which the tea utensils are arranged. The tea utensils include not only those things employed in preparing and serving the tea, but also the items used to decorate the room. In combination, the delicately wrought tea utensils create the placid, serene atmosphere necessary for the tea gathering.

CHARCOAL-ARRANGING UTENSILS A charcoal fire is laid either in the sunken hearth or in the portable brazier, depending on the season. During a formal tea gathering the charcoal will be rearranged twice. In rearranging the charcoal, there are a number of utensils employed. Shown below at right is (from right) the *sumitori* (charcoal container), which is usually made of woven bamboo lined with lacquered paper. The charcoal container holds two kinds of charcoal cut to specific sizes and shapes, depending upon whether a sunken hearth or a portable brazier is being used. The charcoal is arranged in a set pattern in the container. The long, white sticks are charcoal made from azalea branches and painted with gesso. The black charcoal is made from any of a variety of woods. Below the charcoal basket are placed the metal rings *(kan)* that are inserted in the lugs of the kettle when moving it on and off the fire. The large feather *(haboki)* is used to dust the brazier or hearth frame when rearranging the charcoal. The metal chopsticks *(hibashi)* are for transferring and arranging the charcoal, and adding incense to the fire. The incense container *(kogo)* is placed to the lower left of the brazier. Not shown is the *kamashiki,* or trivet used when the kettle is removed from the fire.

   Also used in rearranging the charcoal are the ash container *(haiki)* and the ash spoon *(haisaji),* both shown below at left. When a portable brazier is used, the ash container holds white ash made from the woody stem of the wisteria plant, while for a sunken hearth it contains the same kind of ash as is used to line the hearth.

KETTLE   Water is heated for tea in a *kama* (kettle). The phrase "to put on a kettle" is sometimes used to mean to hold a tea gathering. The kettle has two lugs, or protuberances, on each side. Metal rings are inserted in these so that the kettle can be lifted; the lugs of a kettle used for a portable brazier are placed slightly lower on the kettle than are those of one used with a sunken hearth. During the Muromachi period (1336–1568) these kettles were manufactured mainly in Ashiya near Kobe, while in the Momoyama period (1568–1603) they came to be made in Kyoto as well. Today such kettles are made in Yamagata and Niigata prefectures and the cities of Morioka and Kanazawa. The sound of the water simmering in a kettle is called *matsukaze,* the sighing of the wind blowing through pine trees. There are said to be six different tones of this sound. Kettles come in a wide variety of shapes and sizes.

PORTABLE BRAZIER AND SUNKEN HEARTH For practitioners of tea, the year is divided into two seasons: that of the sunken hearth *(ro)*, which lasts from November through April, and that of the portable brazier *(furo)*, which lasts from May through October. A tea gathering held in November is called *kairo,* or changing of the sunken hearth, and that held in May is *shoburo,* or first portable brazier.

Use of the portable brazier is said to date back to the Kamakura period (1185–1336). At that time braziers were made of iron, although today they are also made of clay or bronze. The bed of ash in the brazier is an object of appreciation and is therefore carefully shaped by the host both for its beauty and to ventilate the charcoal fire.

The kettle used on a brazier is somewhat smaller than that used in the sunken hearth. When a brazier is used, the utensils should be selected to harmonize with it: for example, a bamboo basket suggesting a cool feeling is often used as a flower container during brazier season.

Throughout the year there are many special occasions for tea gatherings. For example, a tea gathering is often held on Children's Day, May 5. This was formerly called Boys' Festival or the Feast of Irises. For this occasion, suitable utensils might be a water container with a pattern of carp, an incense container with the design of a quiver on it, and a tea scoop with the poetic name "Iris-shaped Sword."

On July seventh there is the Star Festival. During November there is *kuchikiri,* the opening of the storage jar that contains the year's new tea. A special tea gathering to taste the new tea is one of the highlights of the year. In December the end of the year is often marked with a tea gathering, and New Year's is celebrated with *hatsugama,* the first tea gathering of the year. *Setsubun,* the last day of the year according to the lunar calendar, comes in early February and is a suitable occasion for a tea gathering. In March, the *gotoku* (iron trivet) is often removed from the sunken hearth and a tea gathering is held in which the kettle is hung on a chain from the ceiling. In April a special kettle is rested on the edge of the sunken hearth; for this, the kettle used is a little lighter in weight than is usual and pieces of wood are placed at two points of contact between the kettle and the sunken hearth. In addition to these special occasions, a tea gathering can be held any time the host desires. There are many kinds of tea gatherings throughout the year, each with its own characteristics, each creating its own atmosphere and feeling.

Pictured here are two types of portable braziers and two sunken hearths, one with a kettle set in it and one with the kettle hanging from a hook. The sunken hearth is surrounded by a lacquered wooden frame called a *robuchi.*

RINSE-WATER CONTAINER After a tea bowl has been rinsed, the used water is poured into the rinse-water container *(kensui)*. The container is made of bronze, wood, or pottery.

LID REST The lid rest *(futa-oki)* is used to support the lid of the kettle when it is removed from the fire. It can be made of bamboo, porcelain, bronze, or iron, although bamboo is the most common material. If a sunken hearth is used, there should be a node in the middle of the bamboo rest; if a portable brazier is used, the node should be at the upper end of the rest.

TEA SCOOP The tea scoop (*chashaku*) is usually made of bamboo, although occasionally ivory or plain or lacquered wood is used. Scoops without a node in the handle are called *shin* type; those with a node in the middle of the handle are *so* type; and those with a node at the end of the handle are the *gyo* type. Most scoops are usually of the *so* type. The artisan who crafts the scoops will usually give a specific poetic name to each, such at "Outgoing Boat," "Incoming Boat," "Spring Wind," "Firefly," "Demon's Arm" and so on. The name of the scoop being used often enhances the theme of a particular tea gathering. Tea scoops, which are highly valued, are carefully stored in containers that are signed by the individual who made each scoop. Occasionally a tea master will also sign a container, indicating his high appreciation for that particular tea scoop.

TEA WHISK   The bamboo whisk used to whip the tea and make it frothy is called the *chasen*. Since the early sixteenth century, the best tea whisks have come from the Nara region. Many kinds of bamboo can be used in making these whisks. Each whisk is made from a single piece of bamboo that has been carefully split and then tied with thread.

WATER LADLE   The bamboo ladle *(hishaku)* is used to dip water out of the kettle and the water jar. The ladle used with a sunken pit *(top)* is larger than that used with a portable brazier *(bottom)*.

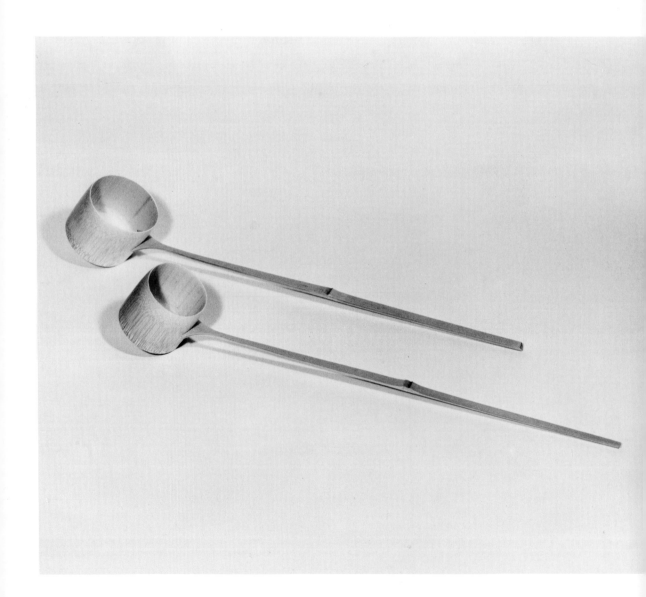

WATER CONTAINER   The water container *(mizusashi)* is usually brought into the room at the beginning of the procedure for making tea. The container can be made of any of a variety of materials, including porcelain, metal, bamboo, or wood.

CONTAINER FOR THICK TEA   Two kinds of tea are used at formal tea gatherings: *koicha,* or thick tea, and *usucha,* or thin tea. Thick tea is served at the most formal part of the tea gathering. The container for thick tea is called a *cha-ire* and is usually ceramic with an ivory lid. The underside of the lid is lined with gold foil: tradition has it that the gold foil will turn color if there is any poison in the tea, a situation that many of Japan's great historical figures feared. The cha-ire is displayed in a small silk bag *(shifuku)* when it is not being used. Old cha-ire are called *karamono,* meaning that they either were made in China during the T'ang period (617–907) or are cha-ire similar in style to these, but made in Japan from clay and glaze brought from China by Kato Toshiro, who supposedly studied ceramics there around 1220. The cha-ire made from Japanese materials are called *wamono.* Those wamono made during the Muromachi period (1336–1568) in the Seto region are called *Ko-seto.* During the Momoyama (1568–1603) and Edo (1603–1868) periods, wamono were produced in the Karatsu, Takatori, Bizen, Satsuma, Tamba, Zeze, and Shigaraki regions. Shown at right are four different types of containers for thick tea. The *katatsuki* (shouldered) shape pictured at the upper right is the most common type. Shown below are various kinds of silk bags.

CONTAINER FOR THIN TEA The tea containers used for thin tea are called *usuchaki* or *usuki*. These are usually lacquerware, often with a gold design, although they can be ceramic or made from wood, bamboo, or lacquered papier-mâché.

INCENSE AND INCENSE CONTAINER There are two general types of incense used at tea gatherings: aromatic woods and *neriko,* a paste blended of aromatic ingredients. There are also two general kinds of incense containers, according to the materials used in making them: non-ceramic, usually lacquered-wood containers decorated with carvings or a lacquered pattern, or inlaid with mother-of-pearl or metal; and ceramic containers, the most representative being Chinese ware decorated with underglaze cobalt. Incense made from aromatic wood is placed in non-ceramic containers and neriko in ceramic containers. At a tea gathering where the fire is built before the guests arrive, the incense container is put on display in the tokonoma.

TEA BOWL   Tea bowls *(chawan)* for tea gatherings were originally imported to Japan from the Asian mainland. In the fifteenth century the famous *Temmoku chawan* were introduced from China, and later the Korean-made *Ido chawan* came to be widely used in Japan. In the latter part of the sixteenth century, many Korean ceramists came to Japan and settled in the Karatsu, Takatori, and Hagi regions, where they made pottery for tea gatherings. Sen Rikyu preferred tea bowls made by the ceramist Chojiro (1516–92); even today, his descendants produce tea bowls, known as *Raku chawan,* for gatherings. Tea bowls for thick tea are usually unfigured and heavier and more solid than those used for thin tea; *Raku chawan* and *Ido chawan* are the most popular kinds of bowls for thick tea.

HANGING SCROLL   Usually there will be a hanging scroll in the tokonoma of both the waiting room and the tearoom. These can be either calligraphic or pictorial. The two scrolls will be related in such a way as to add to the theme of the particular tea gathering that is being held. From the top of the scroll hang two small strips of fabric bonded to paper; these are called *futai,* or wind

strips. If these stir, it means that the air currents in the room are too strong and the scroll should be taken down or it might be torn.

How is the hanging scroll used to help evoke a certain mood for a tea gathering? The hanging scroll in the waiting room, for example, may depict a scarecrow standing in the middle of a rice paddy and holding a bow and arrow, while being blown by a very strong wind. The calligraphy in the tearoom, then, may make reference to the first hanging scroll by stating that not even a bit of cloud can be seen in the infinite expanse of the sky. For the refined Japanese, this combination of painting and calligraphy will signify the coming of autumn, since in Japan blue skies appear in October after storms in September.

FLOWERS FOR A TEA GATHERING

Chabana (flowers for a tea gathering) are a simple but elegant decoration for the tokonoma. Unlike the more complicated ikebana for which Japan is famous, a flower arrangement for a tea gathering usually consists of one or two flowers and a single branch with a few leaves. The containers used for these simple arrangements are made from a wide variety of materials: copper, porcelain, unglazed pottery, bamboo, and so on. Some containers are hung from a hook in the wall or the pillar of the tokonoma, or from its ceiling, while others are placed on its floor. Although there are no prescribed techniques for placing these flowers in the container, it takes an experienced, sensitive eye that can tell which flowers and leaves are unnecessary and should therefore be removed if the arrangement is to be light and airy and thus best capture the beauty of the moment. But more than technical skill is necessary: the best arrangements are not designed by the eye and hands alone, but rather are made by the sincere heart of the host.

The guests at a tea gathering should not only appreciate the flowers for their beauty, but should also sense the transience of human existence as they contemplate the flowers' short life. The flowers and greenery used should be appropriate to the season and be placed in the container as if they were still in the field, for this will best contribute to the mood of the tea gathering. Those flowers gathered in the morning while they are just beginning to open are especially suited to the tea setting. In preparing for a tea gathering, the host will often search far and wide for the flowers he will place in the tokonoma.

Following are shown tea-gathering flower arrangements appropriate to the months of the year.

JANUARY Camellia bud and ornamental kale with wild greenery in a two-tiered bamboo container with a gold-on-black lacquer design of tortoises and waves on the inside. This container is hung on the pillar of a tokonoma.

FEBRUARY Red camellia in a gourd-shaped yellow Seto-ware container hung on the wall of a tokonoma.

MARCH Camellia and wildflowers in a Kainei-ware container placed on the floor of a tokonoma.

APRIL Forsythia and camellia in a Seto-ware container hung on a tokonoma pillar.

 JANUARY▲　　　▼MARCH

FEBRUARY▲　　　▼APRIL

MAY Chrysanthemum, thistle, and other wild-flowers in a woven bamboo basket placed on the floor of a tokonoma.

JUNE Wild lily and aster in a Hagi-ware container on a black-lacquered board placed on the floor of a tokonoma.

JULY Wild grasses and flowers in a woven bamboo basket placed on the floor of a tokonoma.

AUGUST Rose of Sharon and wild grass in a bronze container on a blacklacquered board.

SEPTEMBER Rose of Sharon and arrowroot in an Agano-ware container hung from the ceiling of a tokonoma.

OCTOBER Chrysanthemum and an autumn branch in a bamboo container hung from the ceiling of a tokonoma.

NOVEMBER Camellia and wild shrubbery in a bamboo container on a burnt-cedar board placed on the floor of a tokonoma.

DECEMBER Camellia in a copper vase on a red-lacquered tray placed on the floor of a tokonoma.

COMBINATION AND ARRANGEMENT OF UTENSILS The atmosphere created for a tea gathering depends largely upon the host's skillful combination and arrangement of the utensils to be used. Let us look, for example, at a superb combination for a tea gathering on a hot summer day. On a portable brazier, a small kettle emits *matsukaze,* the sound of the winds sighing in the pines. In the tokonoma hangs a picture of a waterfall. To the left of this hangs a flower basket shaped like a *natazaya,* a hatchet sheath made of bamboo and used by woodcutters of old. A clematis vine, topped by a white flower, stretches from this up toward the painting. In the right-hand corner of the tokonoma sits a red-lacquered incense container with a relief of an angler on it. The use and placement of this container indicate that the charcoal fire has already been laid, and its design evokes the image of an angler fishing in the stream at the bottom of the waterfall in the picture.

The water container set by the brazier is shaped like a well bucket, and the thin-tea container of gold lacquer has a design of green maple leaves. The tea bowl has a picture of Mount Fuji, its summit covered with snow. The tea scoop, made of a dark-colored bamboo, is named Mountain Wind, evoking the idea of a wind that blows down from the snowy mountain, over the waterfall, and through the clematis and maples. For the guests, the overall atmosphere created is that of sitting by a cool stream while a refreshing breeze blows down from the mountain. In the midst of a hot summer's day, one feels tranquil and restored.

In the case of a winter tea gathering, one might see a wide-mouthed kettle steaming on the sunken hearth. The calligraphy in the tokonoma reads: "A flake of snow on the warm fire in the hearth." The tokonoma also holds a bamboo flower vase with a camellia and an incense container shaped like a butterbur flower. The tea container has a design of plum blossoms and a half moon. This combination and arrangement suggest that spring is quickly approaching, while the calligraphy of the hanging scroll alludes to the transitory nature of life.

4

REFRESHMENTS

THICK TEA AND THIN TEA   The distinctions between the two types of powdered tea used at a tea gathering begin with the color of the leaves from which the tea is made: those leaves that are vibrant bluish-green in color are ground for thin tea, while the dark purplish-green leaves are used for thick tea. The difference in color is due to many factors: the amount of sunlight allowed on the plant, the type of fertilizer used, and the methods of handling the freshly picked leaves. But generally speaking, the leaves from the upper portion of the tea plant are used to make thick tea, while those from the lower portion are used for thin tea. In addition, there is a difference in the way that the leaves for each are prepared: after they have been picked, steamed, and dried, those that are used for thick tea are ground more finely than are those used for thin tea.

The two kinds of tea are also distinguished by the kind of tea container in which each is stored, the strength of the tea they make, and the manner in which the tea is served. Thick tea, usually the sweeter of the two, is considered to be the more formal. When it is to be served at a tea gathering, it is stored in a thick-tea container *(cha-ire)*. When making thick tea, three scoopfuls (about 3.5 grams) of the powdered tea are used per guest. At a tea gathering, thick tea is served to all guests, one bowl being shared among them. The host must therefore prepare in that one bowl the exact amount of tea needed so that each guest can take about three-and-a-half sips before passing the bowl on to the next guest.

Thin tea is stored in a thin-tea container *(usuchaki)*. The amount of tea used to make thin tea varies according to the taste of each guest, although one-and-a-half to two scoopfuls is usual. Each bowl of thin tea is individually prepared and served to each guest. Pictured below is a bowl of thin tea.

JAPANESE SWEETS   The type of Japanese sweets *(wagashi)* served at a tea gathering is often chosen to correspond with or evoke the season of the year. If, for example, a light green confection called *shitamoe* (sprouts underneath) is served, the guest will feel that spring is drawing near, even though outside there may still be frost on the ground. If cherry blossoms are in bloom, the sweets may be shaped and colored like fallen cherry petals or fresh foliage, suggesting the end of spring and the greens of early summer.

The sweets, which are eaten before the tea is drunk, both enhance the taste of the tea and augment the beauty of the gathering. Whatever the season or occasion, the host will probably take as much time and care in deciding which sweets will be served as he will in selecting the tea utensils to be used.

There are two general categories of sweets: *namagashi* (fresh, moist sweets), which are served after the kaiseki meal to prepare the palate for thick tea; and *higashi* (dry sweets), which are served with the thin tea.

Usually there are two or three kinds of dry sweets. Each guest will take one of each and place them on a sheet of *kaishi,* the folded pad of white paper that can be used as a napkin. Moist sweets are either served individually on fine plates or in tiered lacquered boxes, or arranged in a bowl from which each guest takes one. In either case, the guest is expected to finish all the sweets he has taken before the tea is served. If he is unable to eat them all, he should take home whatever remains, wrapping these in a sheet of paper from his folded pad.

On the following pages are pictured first moist sweets and then dry sweets appropriate to each of the twelve months of the year.

JANUARY   *Hanabira-mochi* (flower petal) sweets. These are served by the Grand Tea Master of the Urasenke school at the first tea gathering of the new year. They are made of a round piece of rice dough layered with a pink-tinted, diamond-shaped piece of the same and filled with miso and two long slices of steamed burdock.

FEBRUARY *Umegoromo* (plum robe) sweets. In Japan, although trees may still be laden with snow, plum blossoms appear in February, holding the promise of spring. These sweets, decorated with a plum-blossom design, are made of rice dough with a filling of strained red-bean paste.

MARCH *Hitchigiri* sweets. Dainty shreds of colored bean paste are placed on patties of dough made of rice mixed with mugwort. They resemble the shells used in a game played by young girls on March 3, the Doll Festival.

APRIL *Hanakurenai* (pink flower) sweets. These suggest spring, with the green of willows and the pink of cherry blossoms. They are made of delicately tinted white-bean paste.

MAY *Karagoromo* (Chinese robe) sweets. May is the month of irises in Japan. For these sweets, white-bean paste has been wrapped in rice dough that has been partly tinted a faint purple.

JUNE *Mizumo no hana* sweets. Green-tinted bean paste wrapped in arrowroot dough and folded into a three-sided pyramid.

JULY *Mizubotan* sweets. Pink-tinted bean paste wrapped in arrowroot dough mirrors the beauty of the *botan* (tree peony).

FEBRUARY

MAY

MARCH

APRIL

JUNE

JULY

AUGUST

AUGUST *Takenagashi* sweets. Served chilled, these sweets of gelatin, sugar, and red-bean paste mixed and packed into green bamboo offer a cooling respite from the heat of the summer.

SEPTEMBER *Kohagi-mochi* (bush clover) sweets. Bush clover is one of the so-called seven grasses of autumn in Japan. Its pink blossoms and green leaves are reflected in the design of these rice-dough sweets.

OCTOBER *Minori no aki* (autumn harvest) sweets. These sweets, made of mashed sweet potato topped with pieces of boiled chestnut, are dyed and shaped to evoke the autumn foliage of a mountain.

NOVEMBER *Konoma no nishiki* (autumn brocade) sweets. The last leaves of autumn form a brilliant brocade on the mountains. For these sweets, white-bean paste is wrapped in rice dough and sprinkled with ground poppy seeds, calling to mind the frost on the late-autumn trees.

DECEMBER *Kazabana* (snowflake) sweets. Gently falling snowflakes resemble flower petals being scattered by the wind. A steamed sweet filled with red-bean paste and stamped with the design of a snowflake.

NOVEMBER

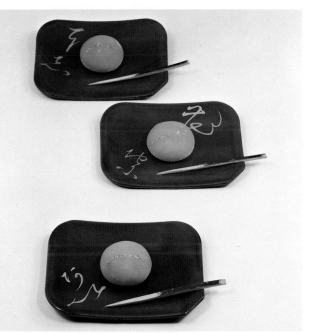

SEPTEMBER

OCTOBER

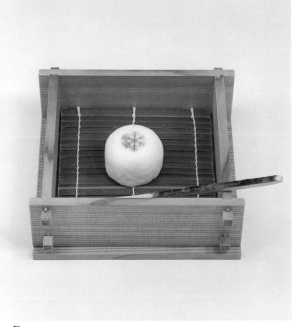

DECEMBER

JANUARY, UPPER RIGHT: *Wakamatsu* (young pine) sweets. Young pine trees symbolize the hopes for the new year. For these sweets, the impression of a pine branch is stamped on soft rice crackers, which are then stacked, with miso placed between each layer. LOWER LEFT: *No-shimusubi* (gift knot) sweets. At New Year's, gifts of money are often wrapped in strips of paper. These sweets, similar to ribbon candy served in the West, are made of strips of sugar cake that have been dyed red and white, the traditional congratulatory colors in Japan, and tied in knots before they harden.

FEBRUARY, UPPER RIGHT: *Otafuku* sweets. Ground soybeans and sugar are mixed and pressed into a mold to produce this image of a happy but plain-looking woman with enormous cheeks. She is traditionally called Otafuku. LOWER LEFT: *Neji-ribo* sweets. Sugar cakes are tinted and twisted to represent the pull ropes on bells at Shinto shrines. February is the first month of the lunar new year, so congratulatory colors and symbols are once again used.

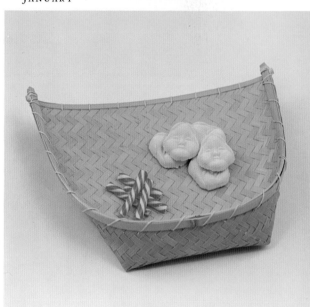

MARCH, UPPER RIGHT: *Kocho* (butterfly) sweets. The first butterfly, heralding spring. These are sugar cakes pressed into a mold. LOWER LEFT: *Sawarabi* (bracken sprout) sweets. Sugar cakes cut and shaped like the bracken sprouts that appear in early spring.

APRIL *Kompeito* (star) sweets. April is a time of cherry-blossom-viewing picnics, and these tiny sugar cakes are often used when serving tea outdoors with special utensils. These were originally brought to Japan by the Portuguese.

MAY, UPPER RIGHT: *Kutsuwa* (horse bit) sweets. These sugar cakes are shaped like the old-style bits used for horses in Japan. LOWER LEFT: *Tazuna* (bridle) cakes. Sugar cakes dyed and twisted to resemble the old-time bridle for a horse.

JUNE, UPPER RIGHT: *Taki-sembei* (waterfall crackers). Sugar cakes pressed to look like a waterfall flowing down. LOWER LEFT: *Aokaede* (maple bud) sweets. Sugar cakes in the form of new maple leaves in the spring.

JULY, UPPER RIGHT: *Tombo* (dragonfly) sweets. The image of this summer insect is pressed into the top of these sugar cakes. LOWER LEFT: *Uzu* (water-eddy) sweets. Sugar cakes twisted to look like cooling eddies of water.

AUGUST, UPPER RIGHT: *Omodaka* (water plantain) sweets. Cakes of raw sugar are shaped to resemble the water plantain that blooms in summer. LOWER LEFT: *Kanzemizu* sweets. Raw sugar pressed into the form of water ripples.

SEPTEMBER, UPPER RIGHT: *Ko-imo* (taro) sweets. Raw sugar is shaped like the young taro, which is harvested in the fall. LOWER LEFT: *Imo no ha* (potato leaf) sweets. Raw sugar is formed to simulate the leaves of the taro plant.

54 REFRESHMENTS

OCTOBER

NOVEMBER

DECEMBER

OCTOBER, UPPER RIGHT: *Naruko* (bird clapper) sweets. These baked rice crackers are shaped like the boards used for clappers that scare off birds from eating the rice that is ready for harvest; the images of three pieces of bamboo, which act as the clappers, are branded on the surface. LOWER LEFT: *Suzume* (sparrow) sweets. Hard-sugar cakes in the abstract form of sparrows darting around an autumn field.

NOVEMBER, RIGHT: *Icho* (gingko leaf) sweets. Sugar cakes colored and pressed to resemble the golden glory of the gingko leaf in autumn. LEFT: *Shimeji* (mushroom) sweets. Sugar cakes colored and shaped like mushrooms.

DECEMBER, UPPER RIGHT: *Yukiwa* (snowflake) sweets. Sugar cakes pressed into the form of snowflakes. LOWER LEFT: *Sasamusubi* (bamboo-grass knot) sweets. Along mountain paths in the winter, bamboo grass can be seen beneath the snow. These sugar cakes are shaped and colored to resemble leaves of bamboo grass tied in knots.

KAISEKI CUISINE   *Kaiseki* is a light meal served at the beginning of a formal tea gathering. *Kai* means "bosom" and *seki* means "stone." The word derives from the former practice by Buddhist novitiates of holding warmed stones to their stomachs in order to alleviate both their hunger and coldness. The word "kaiseki" thus indicates a light meal that, like a warmed stone, barely satisfies one's hunger.

The kaiseki menu consists of *mukozuke* (food to be eaten with sakè), white rice, miso soup, *nimono* (cooked delicacies in a broth), *yakimono* (broiled fish, meat, fowl, and/or vegetables), *hashi-arai* or *kosuimono* (a light broth), *hassun* (a small tray of two delicacies, one from the mountains or fields and the other from the ocean), Japanese pickles, and crisp browned rice served with hot water. Sakè accompanies the whole meal. The menu for formal Japanese dinners, as well as the proper manners and etiquette for eating such meals, evolved from this kaiseki cuisine.

One of the most important elements in kaiseki cuisine is that it be artistically displayed and served. The host will therefore exert great thought and effort in selecting the ingredients and utensils to be used, and must make sure that each dish is the best of its kind and is served at the proper temperature. The guest, in turn, should realize the care and concern that the host has taken and admire the appearance and taste of each dish while observing the proper etiquette when eating the meal.

A central factor in a tea gathering is stimulation of the sense of taste. The five basic tastes—sweet, sour, bitter, spicy, and salty—are all therefore represented in the formal tea gathering. The bitterness of the green tea is complimented by the sweets. The food eaten with sakè is sour, and mustard is added to the miso soup to make it spicy. The broiled fish is usually seasoned with salt.

Immediately after a date has been set for a tea gathering, the prospective host will turn his attention to planning the menu, taking into consideration the ages of the guests and their culinary preferences. As a rule, the host will choose a food that is in season. Sometimes he will, as a compliment, choose something from the native area of the principal guest.

The mukozuke, white rice, and miso soup are served together on a tray. Below, the mukozuke consist of thin layers of sea bream stacked with seaweed, sea-hare eggs, boiled chrysanthemum flower, and Japanese horseradish, all served in a square blue-and-white dish. The soup, served in a covered, black-lacquered bowl, contains a cake of wheat gluten and seaweed, a piece of the meat of a gourd, and mustard.

1

1. The bowl of cooked delicacies in a broth features a shrimp dumpling, mushrooms, a spinach sprout, and slices of citron, all in a red-lacquered bowl decorated with a pattern of chrysanthemums and water.

2. The *yakimono*, broiled harvest fish on a handled pottery plate.

3. Extra dishes are sometimes served along with the traditional ones. For example, the pottery dish in the upper right holds dried tofu that has been cooked, and broiled quail-meat patties topped with shredded citron. The other dish holds a mixture of chopped ark shell, cockle, and endive, with shredded icicle radish.

4. Covered lacquered bowls and tray used for serving the light broth.

5. Iron-and-brass sakè decanter and *hassun* tray with cooked gingko nuts (upper right) and slices of dried mullet roe (lower left).

6. Lacquered hot-water container holding crisp browned rice and hot water, on a tray with a ladle and a dish of Japanese pickles.

4

2

3

5

6

TENSHIN REPAST   *Tenshin* is a light repast, rather than a formal meal like kaiseki
cuisine. Served in a box or basket or on a tray,
tenshin usually consists of white rice, sashimi,
and/or broiled fish, vegetables, and Japanese
pickles. Although if the same courses were served
in separate dishes and bowls, this could be called
kaiseki cuisine, tenshin is used for less formal tea
gatherings or for those to which a large number
of guests have been invited. Other, simpler types
of food, such as buckwheat noodles with condi-
ments, may also be served as tenshin.

5

A TEA GATHERING

There are two basic types of tea gatherings: that in which a portable brazier is used and that in which a sunken hearth is used. The following step-by-step explanation of a tea gathering is based upon one in which a portable brazier is used in a four-and-a-half mat room on an afternoon during the warm season of the year. It is a description of a standard tea gathering, although space does not permit every detail to be explained in full. Circumstances may not always allow one to remain completely true to the standard when participating in a tea gathering, but adaptations should always be made with this model in mind. Three guests have been invited to this tea gathering. As will be seen, the principal guest (who might also be considered the guest of honor) plays a central role, for during much of the tea gathering he is the only spokesman between the guests and the host; usually he is also the guest who is most knowledgeable in the procedures of a tea gathering. The last guest also plays an important part, for he must know where and when utensils are to be set and moved. During the tea gathering, the host does not join the guests during the eating and drinking, except for exchanging some cups of sakè; he is there to serve the guests, for whom the gathering is being held.

INVITATION   There are different types of tea gatherings according to time of day, season, occasion, and so on. When invited to a tea gathering, one of the first things to determine is what kind of tea gathering it will be: a formal one with kaiseki cuisine, one with a light tenshin snack, or an *oyose*, a tea gathering to which many guests are invited. Then one must determine the purpose of the tea gathering: commemorative, memorial, or some other special occasion.

It is important to pay attention to the hour at which the gathering will be held, for the kind of tea gathering also varies according to time of day. For example, an *akatsuki chaji* (dawn tea gathering) begins at about 4 A.M. and is held usually in February or March. An *asa chaji* (morning tea gathering that starts at about 6 A.M.) is held in the cool of a summer morning. A *yobanashi chaji* begins between 6 and 7 P.M. and is held during the winter. In addition, there are many other types of tea gatherings according to time of day and season.

After receiving an invitation, the guest should reply immediately, making a *zenrei* (visit in advance) by which the guest pays a call on the host to accept the invitation, rather than sending a written reply. Among other things, this gives the guest the chance to see exactly where the gathering is to be held and how long it will take to get there, for it is especially important that a guest be punctual when attending a tea gathering. For example, if it is to begin at 11 A.M., the guest should arrive at the site for the tea gathering at about 10:45. If water has already been sprinkled around the entrance gate when he arrives, the guest may enter. The guest should be neither too late nor too early, for the host begins to cook the rice and soup only when all the guests have arrived. Thus, one guest being late can greatly inconvenience the host.

WHAT TO WEAR A Japanese tea gathering is a display of specific customs and manners held in a Japanese-style room. For this reason, it is best to wear a kimono. The participants in a tea gathering contribute to its harmonious atmosphere and beauty through the grace of their movements, which are complemented by the shape and cut of a kimono. For certain occasions, such as a memorial service, the color and pattern of a kimono are carefully prescribed, but in most instances good taste and common sense should guide the guest when choosing what to wear. Whatever the occasion, the guest should select something that will harmonize with the atmosphere of a tea gathering. If a kimono is unavailable, one may wear Western clothing, but in this case it is wise not to wear clothes that fit too tightly at the knees.

ARTICLES TO BE TAKEN When attending a tea gathering, the guest should bring the following items: *(top row, from left)* a slightly dampened and folded white linen cloth *(kochakin)* in a small case, a folded pad of white paper *(kaishi),* and a small pick *(kuromoji)* in a case; *(second row, from left)* a fabric case in which is carried a small piece of fabric *(kobukusa),* usually made of silk and about 16 cm. by 15 cm., and a silk wiping cloth *(fukusa); (bottom)* a white folding fan; the larger fan is used by men and the smaller by women. The sweets at the gathering will be placed on the folded pad of paper and, if the host does not provide a pick, the guest will use the one he has brought with him to eat the sweets. The linen cloth is used to wipe the rim of the tea bowl after drinking thick tea. The small piece of fabric is sometimes employed as a pad on which the guests may place the tea utensils when viewing them or with which guests can hold a hot tea bowl. The folding fan is indispensable when making a formal greeting.

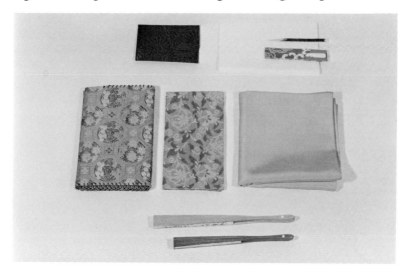

INTRODUCTION

Ise Shrine, the most venerated of all the Shinto shrines in Japan, is approached by a long, quiet road that winds through woods. Walking along this road, one feels purified, especially after a rainfall, when the woods become a variegated pattern of lush greens and the stones glisten underfoot. For a formal tea gathering, the host attempts to create a similar atmosphere and feeling for his guests, so that they too can feel that they are approaching something sacred.

Having completed the preparations for the tea gathering, the host will sprinkle water around the gate and along the garden path. This is done not only to beautify and freshen the garden, but also to inform the guests that the preparations have been made and they may now enter. Seeing that the sprinkling is completed, the guests go into the entryway and from there to the changing room, where they remove their outer garments and change their *tabi,* Japanese split-toed socks. If there is no changing room, these preparations are done in the entryway. Leaving all their belongings except those actually needed for the gathering, the guests then proceed to the waiting room. Upon entering the waiting room, the guests appreciate the decoration, most often a hanging scroll, in the tokonoma; if there is no tokonoma, a scroll may be hung on a folding screen. If there is a calligraphy or painting, it will be something that hints at the theme of this particular tea gathering.

ARRIVAL

1: In the waiting room, the guests take their places after looking at the room's decorations, the principal guest (right) sitting so that the green bamboo tube on the smoking tray that has been provided for the guests is to his right. The *hanto* (host's assistant) brings in small cups of hot water on a tray and invites the guests to drink. **2–3:** After the guests have been served, they bow (*see* page 146) to the host's assistant and then drink.

4–11: When the guests have finished, they go out to the garden, wearing straw sandals that have been provided for them, and proceed to the sheltered waiting arbor. The principal guest goes first, and at the bench he arranges the round, straw cushions for the other guests and himself; once again a tray with smoking utensils is provided.

8 ◀

10 ▶

9 ◀

11 ▶

GREETING BY THE HOST

14

12-15: Soon the host comes out of the teahouse, bringing a bucket of water with him. After first sprinkling water around the stone water basin, he pauses to wash his hands and rinse his mouth. 16–17: He then pours fresh water from the bucket into the basin and carefully places the water ladle on the basin.

12 ◄

15 ▶

13 ◄

16 ▶

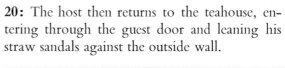

18–19: The host next moves to the middle gate, opens it, and walks toward the waiting arbor. At the same time, all the guests stand up, and the principal guest takes one step forward; the host and the guests bow to each other silently. This signifies that the preparations are complete and the guests are invited to enter the tearoom.

20: The host then returns to the teahouse, entering through the guest door and leaning his straw sandals against the outside wall.

ENTERING THE TEAROOM

21

22

21: After returning to the arbor, all the guests again sit down briefly. **22–24:** Then, after allowing time for the host to return to the teahouse, the principal guest stands, leans his cushion against the back of the bench, bows to the next guest, and proceeds through the middle gate. If there is more than one path in the garden, the host will have placed stones, called *sekimori-ishi* (guard stones), on the first steppingstones of the paths other than the one the guests are to use; this is done so that the guests do not lose their way when proceeding from the bench to the stone water basin. **25–28:** Reaching the basin, the principal guest stoops to wash his hands and rinse out his mouth.

23

24
◀

27
▶

25
◀

28
▶

26

29–32: After completing this ritual purification, the principal guest crouches, opens the sliding wooden door of the guest entrance, places his fan inside the room, slips off his straw sandals, and, still crouching, enters the tearoom. Once inside, the guest stays in a sitting position and turns toward the guest entrance. Reaching down, he picks up his straw sandals and places them leaning against the outer wall so that they are not in the way of the next guest.

30

29
◀

31

33–36: The second guest then proceeds to the tearoom in the same manner.

ENTERING THE TEAROOM 73

37–43: The last guest follows the second guest, straightening the cushions and smoking utensils before leaving the waiting bench and closing the middle gate after him. **44:** After the last guest enters the tearoom, he closes the door with a slight noise, signaling the host, who is in the preparation room, that all the guests have entered the tearoom. **45:** As the guests enter the room, they proceed to the tokonoma, place their fans in front of themselves, and bow toward the hanging scroll. They then silently admire it and bow again. They next go and view the charcoal fire, the kettle, and the portable brazier. Each guest savors the overall atmosphere of the tearoom, observing the play of soft light coming through the papered windows, as well as the slight fragrance of incense that comes from the charcoal fire. Each then takes his place, the principal guest seating himself nearest the tokonoma.

38

37
◄

39

40

41

42

44

43

45

47

48

46–47: Hearing the guests sit down, the host, sitting, opens the *sadoguchi,* the host's entrance connecting the tearoom with the preparation room. (*See* page 150). All guests bow. The host remains sitting there until the principal guest invites him to enter the tearoom. It may seem odd that the guest invites the host, but it should be remembered that the room is now wholly for the guests. **48–49:** The host enters the tearoom and exchanges formal greetings with each guest in turn. Notice how the guests place their folding fans in front of themselves when doing this. **50:** The principal guest, on behalf of all the guests, then makes reference to or asks questions concerning the path, the hanging scroll, and so on. The host answers their questions and then, saying he has made a light meal for them, he goes to the preparation room, closing the door behind him.

46
◄

49

THE KAISEKI MEAL

51

52

51–52: Now the host serves the kaiseki meal. Opening the door again, he sits with a tray in front of him. This tray holds three dishes: two covered lacquer bowls (one containing rice and the other miso soup) and a dish on the far side of the tray holding food to be eaten while drinking sakè. There is also a pair of unfinished cedar chopsticks on the tray.

53–54: The host carries this tray to the principal guest, who slides forward to receive it. The host and principal guest bow in unison. **55:** The principal guest places his tray in front of himself and then bows to the next guest, saying, "Excuse me for being first." **56:** The host then brings in individual trays for the other guests. **57:** After the last guest has been served, the host kneels in the doorway, bows, and says, "Please begin." **58:** Bowing together with the other guests, the principal guest says, "We will begin." **59:** The host then closes the door to the preparation room.

55

53
◄

56
►

54
◄

57
►

58 ◀

▶
60

59 ◀

▶
61

60–62: The second and last guests then say to the principal guest, "We will join you." All three guests lift the lids off their rice and miso-soup bowls at the same time and, after placing the soup-bowl lid on top of the inverted rice-bowl lid, set these to the right side of the tray.

62

63–64: The guests then take up their chopsticks and begin to eat the rice and soup. **65–67:** After the guests have finished their rice and soup, the host opens the door and brings in a container of warm sakè and a stack of sakè cups on a stand. He places these items in front of the principal guest. **68–69:** After bowing to the next guest, the principal guest picks up the stack of cups and, raising them slightly, bows his head in appreciation. **70–72:** He then takes the bottom cup and passes the others on the stand to the next guest.

65 ◀

63 ◀

64 ◀

▶ 66

67 ◀

70 ▶

68 ◀

71 ▶

69 ◀

72 ▶

73–76: As the other guests take their cups, the host pours sakè for the principal guest; he then moves down the line, serving each guest. **77:** After drinking the sakè, the guests sample the food in the dish on the far side of the tray.

75

73 ◄

► 76

74 ◄

► 77

78–80: The host next brings in a container of rice on top of which is placed a small tray holding a large rice scoop. Setting the tray to the side, he opens the lid of the rice container slightly and places the rice scoop inside. The host then asks the principal guest if he may serve him some rice. The principal guest declines, saying that he and the other guests will serve themselves.

79

78 ◀

▶
80

81–82: Picking up the tray, the host then asks the principal guest if he would like more soup; if he desires more, the guest places his covered soup bowl on the tray, and the host carries it to the preparation room to be refilled.

83–85: While the host is out, the principal guest bows to the next guest and then takes the lid off the rice container; the lid is inverted and passed down to the last guest. **86:** The host then returns to collect the second guest's soup bowl; as he does this, the principal guest serves himself

some rice. **87–89:** The principal guest then passes the rice container to the second guest. As this guest serves himself, the host returns with the principal guest's refilled soup bowl. This process continues until all guests have second servings of rice and soup. When the last guest has served himself rice, he places the container on the tatami and puts the lid on it. **90:** Having served the last guest his soup and still sitting in front of him, the host sets the tray he is carrying on top of the rice container. After the host carries these things out, the guests begin to eat their second servings.

85
◀

88
▶

86
◀

89
▶

87
◀

90
▶

91: The host next serves bowls of delicacies in a broth. He first brings in the bowl for the principal guest, carrying it on a round tray. He sets the tray down in front of himself and places the covered bowl in front of the principal guest's tray.   **92:** Then he brings in the bowls for the other guests, carrying these bowls on a large rectangular tray. **93:** After serving the second and last guests, he sits in the doorway and invites the guests to eat the dish before it becomes cold.

91 ◀

92 ◀

93

94–97: The guests all bow to thank him and then pick up the bowls with both hands; they remove the lids, savoring the aroma, and, after putting the lids down, begin to eat. 98: As they enjoy this dish, the host serves them more sakè. After finishing the delicacies in broth, the guests take one sheet from their pad of folded paper and wipe clean the inside of the bowl and lid.

96

94
◀

97
▶

95
◀

98
▶

99–100: Following this, the host brings in a serving dish holding broiled fish (or sometimes meat) with a pair of green bamboo chopsticks. He sets this to the left of the principal guest's tray. **101:** The two bow to each other, the host saying, "Please take some." **102:** After the principal guest takes some of the fish (which he places in the dish on the far side of his tray), he passes the serving dish to the second guest, who then serves himself. **103:** When the last guest has served himself, he sets the serving dish to his left.

101

99

102

100

103

104–5: The host returns with the refilled rice container, tray, and rice scoop, and sets them down in front of the principal guest; he puts the tray to his right, opens the lid slightly, and sticks in the rice scoop. He again asks the principal guest if he may serve him more rice, but the guest again declines, saying that he and the other guests will serve themselves. Holding out his tray, the host then asks the principal guest if he would like more soup, but the principal guest declines, for it is customary not to accept a third bowl of soup.

106: The host goes to the doorway and says, "I will have my meal in the preparation room." **107:** The principal guest replies, "Why don't you join us?" but the host refuses and retires to the preparation room, closing the door as he leaves. The guests then resume eating.

104 ◄

106 ▶

105 ◄

107 ▶

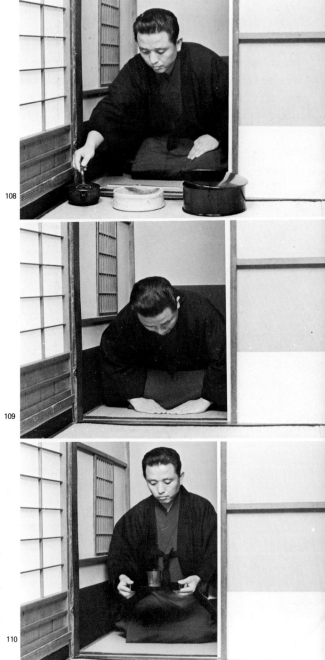

108: After they have finished (taking about fifteen minutes), the last guest places the sakè container, the lidded rice container, and the dish for the broiled fish in front of the door to the preparation room. The host opens the door and removes these items. 109: Bowing in the doorway, he says, "I've finished my meal in the preparation room. I hope you've enjoyed your meal." 110: Next the host brings in a tall, covered bowl holding clear soup made of slightly flavored hot broth; he carries the bowl on the round tray. 111–13: Placing this in front of the principal guest, he sets out the bowl of clear soup and takes the bowl that was used for the delicacies in broth. 114: He then brings in the bowls for the other guests, carrying them on the large rectangular tray, and exchanges these for the bowls that were used for the delicacies in broth. 115–16: The host returns to the doorway, bows, and says, "Please have your soup." The guests all bow and, taking up the soup bowls in both hands, remove the lids and drink the soup.

111 ◀

114 ▶

112 ◀

115 ▶

113 ◀

116 ▶

117: When the guests have finished their soup, the host brings in a small wooden tray, called a *hassun*, holding two stacks (one of ocean delicacies and one of mountain delicacies) of food and green bamboo chopsticks, and the sakè container. 118: He sets these in front of the principal guest and pours a cup of sakè for him. 119: As the principal guest drinks, the host, after asking permission, takes the lid off the bowl of the principal guest's clear soup and places some of the ocean delicacies on the inside of the soup-bowl lid. These are eaten by the principal guest. 120–22: The host then repeats the serving of sakè and ocean delicacies with each guest.

118

119

117
◀

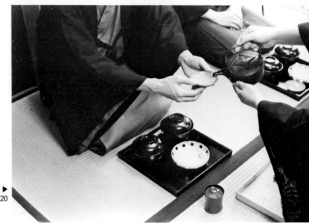

▶
120

121

122

123: After everyone has been served ocean delicacies, the host carries the tray and sakè container back to the principal guest and sits down. The principal guest says, "May I pour sakè for you?" The host replies, "I don't have my own cup. May I use yours?" The principal guest then takes out his pad of folded paper, wipes his cup, and places it on the small lacquer stand on which the host had originally brought in the cups.

▶
123

125

124–25: In the meantime, the host turns the tray, places it to the right of the principal guest's tray, and moves the sakè container toward the second guest, the spout pointing away from the guest. **126:** The host then picks up the cup that the principal guest has just wiped, and the second guest pours some sakè for the host. **127:** As the host drinks this, the principal guest serves him one of each of the delicacies, placing these on a sheet from his pad of folded paper; the host accepts these, but does not eat them. At the same time, the second guest sets the sakè container down, the spout pointing away from the host.

126

124
◄

127

128: After the host has finished his sakè, the second guest asks him if he may borrow the host's cup to drink from. **129:** The host says to the principal guest, "Please let me use your cup for a while." **130:** The host moves toward the second guest, gives him the cup, and pours some sakè for him. The host then places the sakè container near the last guest, takes up the tray of delicacies, and serves the principal guest and the second guest some of the mountain delicacies, placing them on the lids of their clear-soup bowls.

130

128

131: When the host receives the sakè cup back from the second guest, the last guest the pours some sakè for the host. Then the host gives the sakè cup to the last guest and pours for him. As the last guest drinks, the host serves him some of the mountain delicacies. The last guest returns the empty cup to the host, pours more sakè for him, and eats the mountain delicacies.

129
◀

▶
131

132–33: The host wipes the cup, sets it on the cup stand, and places the stand on the tray. Taking up the tray and the sakè container, the host goes back to the principal guest. Sitting, the host says, "Thank you for letting me have the cup for so long," and pours more sakè for the guest.

center of the tray, sets the cup stand on the left-hand side of the tray, and places the sheet of paper with his own uneaten portion of delicacies on the right-hand side. **138:** Picking up the tray and the sakè container, the host takes these items to the preparation room. **139:** The host returns with a rectangular tray on which rests a spouted container holding crisp browned rice and hot water, a ladle, and a dish of Japanese pickles with green bamboo chopsticks. **140–41:** Sitting in front of the principal guest, he places the dish of pickles to the guest's right.

132

133
◄

134

134: The principal guest then pours more sakè for the host. **135:** After the host drinks, the principal guest says, "I have had enough sakè and now I would like some hot water." The host places the cup on the cup stand. **136–37:** The host arranges what is left of the delicacies in the

135

136

▶
139

137

▶
140

138

▶
141

142: Opening the lid of the container slightly, he sets the ladle inside and then places the container near the dish of pickles.   **143–44:** The host collects the bowls for the clear soup from each guest, placing them on the large rectangular tray, and returns with them to the preparation room. **145:** Sitting in the doorway, the host bows and says, "Please let me know if there isn't enough hot water." **146:** The principal guest bows slightly in reply. The host closes the door.

144

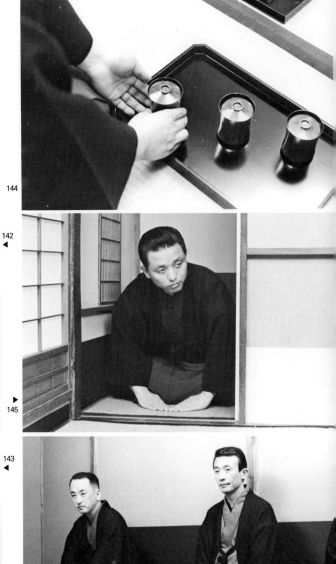

142 ◄

▶ 145

143 ◄

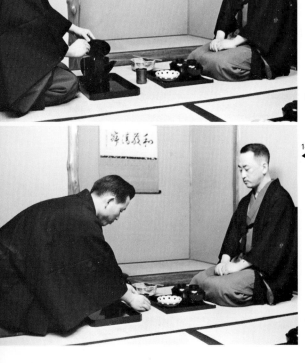

▶ 146

147: The principal guest then takes the lid off the hot-water container and passes it down; the last guest places it to his left. **148–49:** The principal guest next serves himself some pickles, placing them in the dish on the far side of his tray and then passing the dish down. **150–51:** Using the ladle, each guest scoops rice and hot water into both his empty soup bowl and rice bowl, which still contains some rice. Each then pours the mixture from his soup bowl into his rice bowl. They eat the rice and hot water, sampling the pickles at the same time. Everything must be finished, for it is considered impolite to leave any food.

147

149

148

150

151

152: When everything has been eaten, each guest uses paper from his pad of folded papers to wipe his chopsticks and each dish and bowl. **153:** The utensils are then arranged on the tray, with the cover for the rice bowl being replaced upside down so that the inner surface is facing up. The second and last guests, who still have their sakè cups, place these on the lids of their rice bowls. The last guest sets the pickle dish and the container of rice and hot water in front of the door to the preparation room. **154:** When the guests have finished cleaning their utensils, they simultaneously push their chopsticks so that these make a noise falling off the edge of the tray; the host, who remains in the preparation room, hears this sound. **155:** Upon hearing this, the host opens the door and removes the pickle dish and the container of rice and hot water. **156–58:** Next, he enters the room and, bowing to each guest, removes their trays. This ends the kaiseki meal.

153

154

152
◄

155

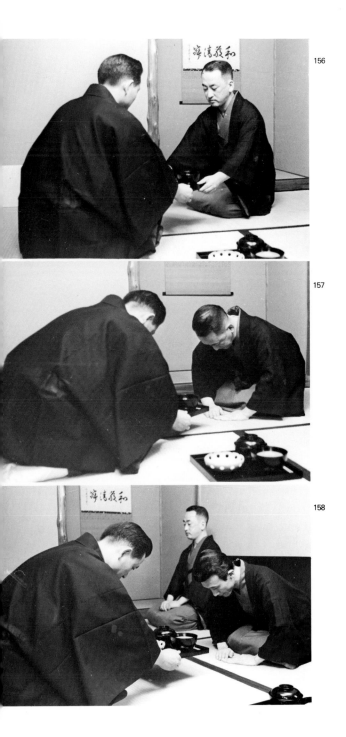

156

157

158

FIRST ARRANGING OF THE CHARCOAL

The first arranging of the charcoal fire follows next. Before the guests arrived, the host had already prepared the brazier itself and started the fire in it. For this, ash had been finely sifted and then placed in the brazier. The ash was then shaped in one of many possible prescribed ways that are designed both for their beauty and to ventilate the charcoal fire. The fire consists of three short sticks of charcoal (*shitabi*) that were lit in the preparation room, carried into the tearoom, and placed on the flat area in the center of the ash. All of this was done well enough in advance so that the coals were glowing and the kettle beginning to steam when the guests arrived. **159:** For the first arranging of the charcoal, the host places the charcoal container so that it will be to his side and in the view of the guests. He then opens the door from the preparation room and bows. The charcoal container is usually made of woven bamboo lined with lacquered paper. In this rest pieces of charcoal of various sizes and shapes; metal chopsticks, with two metal rings hanging from them; and the incense container. On the left-hand side of the rim of the charcoal container lies a large feather brush. **160:** The host sets the basket down to the right of the brazier and brings in the ash container containing a small mound of white ash and the ash spoon, which he sets back to his left. **161–64:** He then removes and arranges all the utensils in the charcoal container in a specific order, places the lid on the kettle securely, and puts the metal rings in the lugs of the kettle. **165:** From the breast of his kimono, the host takes out a thick pad of paper that has been folded in quarters, and places this on the tatami. **166:** Gripping the metal rings firmly, he lifts the kettle off the brazier and sets it on the pad of paper. **167:** He turns to the side and slides the kettle and the pad of paper back to his right. **168:** He then removes the rings and places them on the tatami next to the kettle. **169–70:** He returns to his original position. Using the feather brush, the host next does the first dusting of the brazier, following a set pattern of strokes.

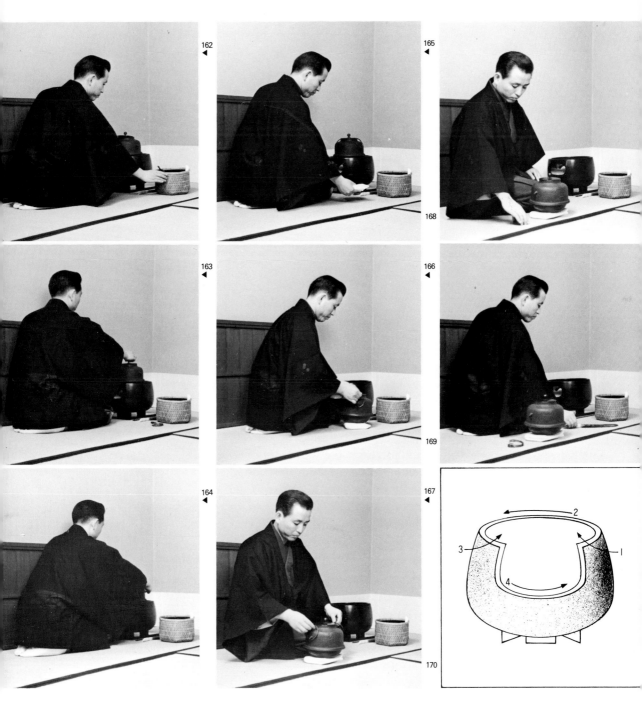

162

165

168

163

166

169

164

167

170

171

172

171–72: The host uses the metal chopsticks to slightly rearrange the charcoal that was earlier placed in the brazier; after this he takes fresh charcoal from the charcoal container and arranges it in the brazier. 173: There is a set pattern in which the charcoal is arranged. 174–75: This is followed by the second dusting of the brazier with the feather brush. 176: Next he picks up the ash container, places it before his knees, and takes the spoon out of it. Using the spoon, he takes one small scoop of ash from the mound of ash in the front of the brazier. By doing this, he destroys the smoothness of the mound that he took so much time and care in shaping. With this act, he is honoring his guests, showing them that it was for them and them alone that this mound of ash was shaped. 177–78: After placing the ash container and spoon behind himself, he does the final dusting of the brazier and places the feather brush on the rim of the charcoal container. 179: The host next picks up the incense container, removes the lid, and, using the metal chopsticks, adds some incense to the fire. He then places the metal chopsticks in the charcoal container. 180–81: As the host places the lid back on the incense container, the principal guest asks him if he and the others may view the container.

173

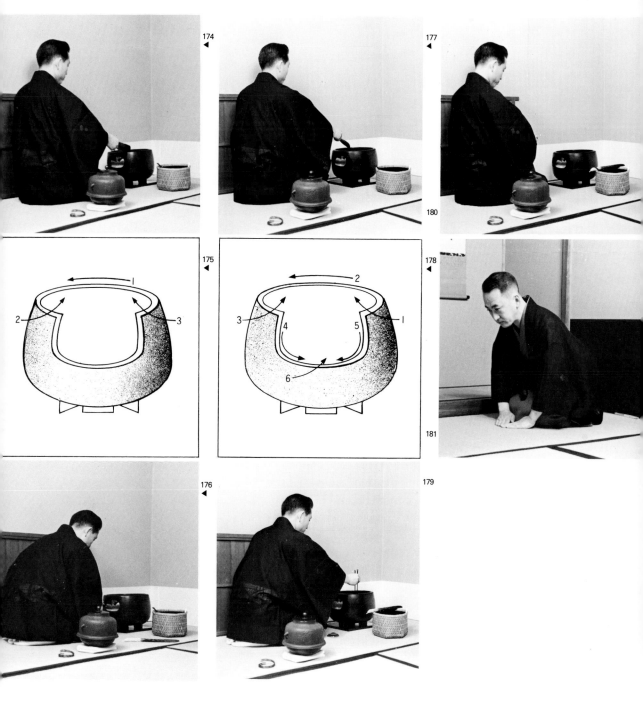

174

175

176

177

178

180

181

179

182: The host, after turning toward the guests, sets the container out for them. **183–85:** The host then puts the kettle back on the brazier, picks up the thick pad of paper, and, after flicking it with his fingers over the charcoal container, places it in his kimono, straightens the kettle, removes the metal rings, places them in the charcoal container, and picks up the ash container and spoon to carry them back to the preparation room. **186:** While the host is out, the principal guest slides forward, picks up the incense container, and slides back to his place. The host then comes and collects the charcoal container. **187:** The host returns to the tearoom with a large feather duster and sweeps the area around the brazier. **188–90:** After that, he retires to the preparation room, sweeping as he goes and closing the door behind him.

185 ◀

▶
188

186 ◀

▶
189

187 ◀

▶
190

191: After the host leaves, the principal guest bows to the second guest and says, "Excuse me while I go first." The principal guest then views the container, passing it on to the next guest when he is through. 192: When the last guest has finished viewing it, he and the principal guest both slide forward. 193: The last guest places the incense container in front of the principal guest and returns to his place. 194: The principal guest replaces the container where the host had set it and then slides back to his place. The host then enters the tearoom, sits in front of the brazier, folds the silk wiping cloth, and wipes the left and right sides of the brazier. Refolding the cloth, he wipes the lid of the kettle and then opens the kettle slightly. He turns so that he is facing the guests. 195: The principal guest compliments the host on the incense container, and asks him about its shape, origin, and so on. After answering these questions, the host takes the incense container to the preparation room. 196: At the preparation-room door he turns, sits, and, putting the incense container down, bows. This ends the first arranging of the charcoal fire.

194

195

196

PARTAKING OF
MOIST SWEETS

198

197–98: The host next comes in with a set of tiered lacquered-wood boxes *(fuchidaka)* containing moist sweets and places the boxes in front of the principal guest; the host then returns to the door of the preparation room, sits, and bows, saying, "Please have these sweets." **199:** The guest bows in reply to this. The host then says he would like to air the room and wants to give the guests a moment to stand. He bows and closes the door. **200:** The principal guest takes one of the boxes for himself and then passes the remaining ones on to the other guests. (*See* page 168.) The guests then eat the sweets, the last guest placing the empty boxes in front of the preparation-room door.

199

197
◀

200

INTERMISSION

After the guests have finished their sweets, following the host's suggestion, there is a short pause, called the *nakadachi,* during which they leave the tearoom and return to the waiting arbor while the host prepares the tearoom for the making and serving of thick tea and thin tea.   **201:** Beginning with the principal guest, each guest views the hanging scroll in the tokonoma and then exits through the guest entrance.

201

202–5: The principal guest arrives first at the waiting arbor and arranges the cushions and smoking utensils. 206: The other guests join him there. 207: While the guests are at the waiting bench, the host sweeps the tearoom and finishes the preparations for serving tea. First he removes the tiered boxes, and then he replaces the scroll hanging in the tokonoma with flowers. Next he brings in the water container and the container for thick tea in its silk bag, setting them down to the right of the brazier.

204

202
◄

205

203
◄

206

207

RETURNING TO THE TEAROOM

In the preparation room, the host sounds a gong to let the guests know that the tearoom is ready.
208: Hearing this, the guests rise from their seats and stoop to the ground; this signifies their humility and the respect that they have for the tea that is to be served.   **209:** The guests take their seats again.   **210–15:** The guests then return to the tearoom, each viewing the flowers in the tokonoma, the kettle, fire, and brazier arrangement, the water container, the thick-tea container, and the silk bag before taking his place.

208

209

210 ◄

213 ▶

211 ◄

214 ▶

212 ◄

215 ▶

217

216–19: The last guest straightens up the cushions and smoking utensils in the waiting arbor and then enters the tearoom, once again closing the door with a slight noise so that the host knows that all of the guests have returned. **220:** Before taking his place, the last guest views the decorations and utensils. **221–23:** When the host hears the last guest close the door, he goes out from the preparation room into the garden, where he removes the ladle from the stone water basin, puts away the cushions and smoking utensils that are in the waiting arbor, and takes down the bamboo blinds that hang in front of the windows of the tearoom. He returns to the preparation room.

218

216
◄

219

220 ◀

▶ 222

221 ◀

▶ 223

PARTAKING OF THICK TEA

224: Making sure that all the guests are seated, the host opens the door to the tearoom. In front of him is set the tea bowl. **225:** Inside this are placed the linen cloth, which has been dampened and folded (*see* page 160), and the tea whisk; on the rim of the tea bowl is set the tea scoop. Resting the bowl on the palm of his left hand and steadying it with his right, he carries it in and arranges it, together with the thick-tea container, in front of the water container. He then returns to the preparation room and brings out the rinse-water container, the lid rest placed inside this and the water ladle laid across the top. **226:** After entering the tearoom, he closes the door behind him. Taking his place, he arranges the lid rest and ladle, and then he and the guests bow in unison. During the preparation and serving of the thick tea, there is no conversation in the room, except for a few words spoken between the host and the principal guest. **227:** After pausing a moment to attain energy and concentration, the host picks up the tea bowl and places it in front of his knees. **228–29:** He then sets the thick-tea container between himself and the tea bowl, and removes the silk bag. **230:** Next he takes the silk wiping cloth from his obi; the host had already folded and secured it in his obi before the guests had come (*see* page 152); he now examines its four edges.

225

224

226
◀

▶
229

227
◀

▶
230

228

231: Refolding the silk wiping cloth, he purifies the thick-tea container and sets it down. **232:** Next he uses the cloth to purify the tea scoop (*see* page 156), setting it on top of the thick-tea container when he is finished. **233:** He removes the tea whisk from the tea bowl and places it next to the thick-tea container. **234:** If the water container lid is lacquered, he will lightly wipe it. **235:** Next the host moves the tea bowl closer to himself and takes the linen cloth out of it, placing the cloth on the lid of the water container. Then he inserts the silk wiping cloth back into his obi. **236:** After picking up the water ladle, he then places the kettle lid on the lid rest at his left, ladles hot water from the kettle into the tea bowl, and returns the ladle with the *oki-bishaku* movement. (*See* page 164.) He places the whisk in the tea bowl. After examining the whisk (*see* page 158), he sets it down, empties the water from the bowl into the rinse-water container, and wipes the tea bowl with the folded linen cloth (*see* page 162), which he then replaces on top of the kettle lid. **237:** Next the host takes up the tea scoop in his right hand and the thick-tea container in his left, removes the container lid, placing it to the right of the tea bowl, and places three large scoops of thick-tea powder in the tea bowl. **238:** After setting the scoop on the rim of the bowl, he holds the thick-tea container over the bowl and turns it to empty the remaining tea from the container into the bowl. The lid is replaced on the tea container and it is set down. The tea scoop is used to level the powder in the tea bowl and then replaced on top of the tea container.

234 ◀

237 ▶

235 ◀

238 ▶

236

239: After taking off the water-container lid, he uses the ladle to transfer some water from the water container to the kettle and then scoops hot water from the kettle into the tea bowl. **240:** He replaces the ladle on the kettle with the *kiri-bishaku* movement. (*See* page 164.) **241:** Taking the whisk in his right hand, the host kneads the tea until it is blended smooth. Pouring hot water over the tines of the tea whisk, he then adds the amount he thinks he will need to thin it to the right consistency; he then finishes making the tea. **242:** Picking up the bowl, he sets it down to his right, with the "front" of the bowl facing the guests. **243:** The principal guest slides forward, picks up the tea bowl, and then slides back to his place. **244:** He sets the bowl between himself and the second guest. Then all the guests bow silently, acknowledging that they will all receive the tea and drink it together. (*See* page 172.) **245:** The principal guest picks up the bowl with his right hand and turns it clockwise twice (180 degrees); this is done so that when the guest drinks, his lips will not touch the "front" of the bowl. The principal guest then raises the bowl and takes a sip, making a slight slurping sound. The host, who is still facing the brazier, turns his head slightly, bows, and asks, "How is the tea?" The principal guest replies, "It is delicious." The host then turns slightly to his right, so that he is facing the guests. The principal guest drinks some more tea, taking his proper share (each guest will take about three and one-half sips). As the principal guest takes his second sip, the second guest bows to the last guest, excusing himself for drinking before the last guest. When the principal guest finishes his tea, he places the

tea bowl in front of his knees and takes his linen cloth out of his kimono to wipe the rim of the bowl where his lips touched it. Finishing this, he puts the cloth back, picks up the bowl, sets it on his left palm, and turns the bowl counterclockwise twice (180 degrees), so that the "front" is once again facing him. **246:** Turning slightly, the principal guest carefully passes the bowl to the second guest.

239

240

241
◀

▶
244

242
◀

▶
245

243
◀

▶
246

247: The second guest takes the bowl, raises it, and bows slightly; at the same time, the principal guest bows. The second guest then drinks the tea as did the principal guest, but there is no exchange between him and the host. However, as the second guest takes his first sip of tea, the principal guest bows to the host, compliments him on the tea, and thanks him. The principal guest then asks what kind of tea it was, and the host replies with the names of both the tea and its packer. Next, the principal guest compliments the host on the sweets he served at the end of the kaiseki meal, and the host bows in acknowledgment. By this time, the second guest has finished drinking the tea, cleaned the bowl, and passed it on to the last guest. The last guest repeats the drinking process, finishing what is left in the bowl. Hearing the last guest making a slurping sound as he finishes the tea, the host turns back to face the brazier; he then transfers a ladle of water from the water container to the kettle, returning the ladle to the kettle with the *hiki-bishaku* movement. (*See* page 164.) At the same time, the principal guest asks the last guest to return the tea bowl to him for viewing. The last guest wipes the bowl and slides forward to give it to the principal guest, setting it down so that the "front" is facing the principal guest. The last guest returns to his place. After saying, "Please excuse me while I go first," the principal guest admires the shape, glaze, and feel of the bowl, as well as the way in which the remnants of the thick, green tea cling to the inside. He then passes it to the second guest. **248– 49:** When the last guest has finished viewing the

bowl, he and the principal guest both slide forward. The last guest places the bowl in front of the principal guest and then goes back to his place. The principal guest returns the bowl to the host, placing it so that the "front" faces the host, and then goes back to his place.

247

248

250: Still facing the brazier, the host takes the bowl and sets it in front of himself. The host and guests all bow in unison.   **251:** The host takes a ladle of hot water from the kettle and pours this into the bowl to rinse it. He returns the ladle to the kettle with the *oki-bishaku* movement and then pours the water from the tea bowl into the rinse-water container.   **252:** The host bows and says, "Please allow me to finish this one procedure." The principal guest bows in reply and at this point may ask the host about the tea bowl.

250
◄

►
252

253: The host then ladles water from the water container into the tea bowl, returns the ladle to the kettle with the *hiki-bishaku* movement and, placing the whisk inside this, rinses and then examines the whisk. Setting the whisk down, he empties the water into the rinse-water container, and places the linen cloth and then the whisk inside the cleaned bowl. **254:** After picking up the tea scoop and moving the rinse-water container back, he takes the silk wiping cloth from his obi and wipes the scoop and then lays it on the rim of the tea bowl. **255:** Next he places the tea bowl slightly to his left. **256:** He then moves the thick-tea container next to the tea bowl, dusts the wiping cloth over the rinse-water container, and secures it in his obi. The host ladles water from the water container into the kettle. **257:** Holding the water ladle, he replaces the lid on the kettle, lays the ladle on the lid rest, and then replaces the lid on the water container. As the lid is set on the water container, the principal guest asks if he and the others may view the thick-tea container, the tea scoop, and the silk bag for the tea container. **258:** After bowing in acknowledgment of the request, the host rests the water ladle on the rinse-water container and places the lid rest behind it. He moves the bowl to the far left. He then picks up the tea container, turns slightly to his right, and, after folding the silk wiping cloth, purifies the container with it. **259:** After this, he sets out the items to be viewed so that they are, in order from the guests' right, the tea container, the tea scoop (curved end

away from the guests), and the silk bag. **260:** The host then turns back toward the brazier and begins to carry out the remaining utensils in the reverse order (the rinse-water container, lid rest, and water ladle; the tea bowl, the linen cloth, and the tea whisk; the water container) from that in which they were brought in.

253

254

255
◄

258
►

256
◄

259
►

257
◄

260
►

261: While the host is taking the rinse-water container out of the room, the principal guest slides forward, picks up the three items that are to be viewed, and slides back, placing them to his right. Having carried out the utensils, the host remains in the preparation room, closing the door behind him when he leaves with the water container.   262: When the host has left, the principal guest bows to the second guest, and says, "Excuse me while I go first."   263–65: The principal guest then examines each item, passing it on to the next guest when he is finished.   266: After all the guests have viewed the items, the last guest and the principal guest both slide forward. The last guest places the items in front of the principal guest and then returns to his place. The principal guest then moves the items so that the tea container will be to the host's right, the tea scoop in the center, and the silk bag to his left. When the principal guest has returned to his place, the host opens the door, enters the room, and sits in front of the items, facing the guests.   267: The principal guest then asks about their provenance, including the poetic name that has been given to the tea scoop. After the host answers these questions, he picks up the items and carries them to the doorway.   268: Placing them near his knees, he and the guests bow; then he closes the door to the preparation room.

264

267

265

268

266 This ends the thick-tea part of the tea gathering. What has occurred may be considered to be the climax of the whole gathering. The preparation and drinking of the tea were carried out in almost complete silence, except for the sounds made by the water, steam, and utensils, plus the minimal conversation between the host and the principal guest. The importance of what follows next—the preparation and drinking of the thin tea—is that it acts as a denouement, helping the guests to get ready for their return to the world that awaits them outside the tearoom.

SECOND ARRANGING
OF THE CHARCOAL

269

270

271

By this time the fire in the portable brazier has begun to die down, so it is necessary to add more charcoal. **269:** Therefore, the host returns to the tearoom with the charcoal-arranging utensils and carries out the second arranging. There are some differences in procedure between this and the first arranging. **270–73:** He first places the lid securely on the kettle and puts the metal rings in the lugs of the kettle. **274–77:** He takes a hot pad out of the charcoal container, puts the kettle on this, slides it back, and removes the metal rings. Then he does the first dusting of the brazier, the arranging of the charcoal, and the second dusting. When he finishes the second dusting, he uses the ash spoon to take some white ash from the ash container and fill in the mark he made in the front of the mound of ash in the brazier during the first arranging of the charcoal. Next he does the final dusting of the brazier. Then, after adding incense to the brazier, the host slides the kettle up toward the brazier and removes the metal rings from the lugs.

272 ◄

► 275

273 ◄

► 276

274 ◄

► 277

278–79: As the host sets the rings down, the principal guest bows and asks if he and the others may view the fire and the brazier. The host takes the ash container and spoon out to the preparation room, where he waits. 280–83: While the host is out, each guest goes in turn to view the fire, brazier, kettle, charcoal container, and charcoal-arranging utensils. 284–85: When the last guest has returned to his place, the host comes in with a *mizutsugi* (spouted water container) that has a damp folded cloth on its lid and, in this example, a lid rest on its spout. 286–87: Sitting in front of the kettle, he puts the kettle lid on the lid rest and adds water to the kettle.

282 ◄

285 ►

283 ◄

286 ►

284 ◄

287 ►

288: After replacing the lid on the kettle, the host wipes the lid and the body of the kettle with the linen cloth; the guests admire the way the steam arises from the surface of the kettle as he does this. **289:** The host then carries out the spouted water container, together with the linen cloth and lid rest. **290–91:** When the host returns, he inserts the metal rings back in the lugs of the kettle and replaces the kettle on the brazier. **292–95:** He then puts the hot pad back in the container, makes sure the kettle is securely set on the brazier, and puts the rings back in the charcoal container. **296–97:** After opening the lid of the kettle slightly, the host carries out the charcoal-arranging utensils, stopping at the host's door to bow to the guests.

289

290

288
◀

291

292
◄

▶
295

293
◄

▶
296

294
◄

▶
297

SECOND CHARCOAL ARRANGING *135*

PARTAKING OF THIN TEA

Now the host brings in a tray with smoking utensils. This indicates that the thin-tea part of the gathering will be much more relaxed than was the thick-tea part; there will probably be more conversation between the host and guests, and among the guests themselves. **298:** The host places the smoking utensils in front of the principal guest and returns to the preparation room. **299:** The principal guest moves the tray of smoking utensils up and to his right. **300:** The host then brings in a tray of dry sweets, which he places in front of the principal guest. After bowing, he goes to the preparation room and starts to bring in the tea utensils. The tea bowl and the container used for thin tea will be different from those used for thick tea, while the other utensils can be the same or differ, according to the wishes of the host. **301–2:** The host first brings in the water container and then the other utensils, carrying them in the same order in which they were brought in for the thick tea, except that the thin-tea container will be brought in with the tea bowl.

298

299 ◄

301 ►

300 ◄

302 ►

303–10: After arranging these, he makes the ³⁰⁴ same preparations as for thick tea. (*See also* page 154.) But thin tea is briskly whisked instead of kneaded so that the surface of thin tea is frothy with tiny bubbles and is lighter in color than is thick tea. **311:** As the host picks up the tea scoop to start making the first bowl of tea, he bows and says to the principal guest, "Please have some sweets." The principal guest takes some and begins to eat. (*See* page 166.) **312:** At the same time, the host prepares the light and frothy thin tea. By the time the principal guest has finished his sweets, the host has prepared the bowl of thin tea and set it out for him.

305

303
◄

306

307
◄

310
▶

308
◄

311
▶

309
◄

312
▶

313: The principal guest slides forward, picks up the bowl, and then slides back to his place. (*See* page 170.) **314:** Setting the bowl between himself and the second guest, he bows and says, "Excuse me while I go first." **315:** He then places the bowl in front of himself and, bowing, says to the host, "I will drink the tea." He picks up the bowl, bows in appreciation, turns it clockwise twice (180 degrees), and drinks. When the principal guest finishes drinking all the tea, he uses his thumb and forefinger (rather than the linen cloth) to wipe the rim of the bowl, afterwards wiping his fingers on the pad of folded paper in his kimono. **316:** He then admires the bowl and slides forward to return it to the host. The host next rinses the bowl and then wipes it with the folded linen cloth. The second guest takes some of the sweets and passes the tray on to the last guest.

314

315

313
◄

316

317: When the second guest finishes his sweets, he slides forward to receive his bowl, returns to his place, and sets the bowl between himself and the principal guest. **318:** Bowing to him, the second guest says, "I'll join you in drinking a cup of tea." **319:** Placing the bowl between himself and the last guest, the second guest bows and says, "Excuse me while I go first." The last guest bows in reply. The second guest then drinks the tea, wipes and views the bowl, and returns it to the host. **320:** After the last guest takes his sweets, he returns the tray to the principal guest. The last guest then has his tea in the same manner as did the first two guests. After the last guest has returned the tea bowl to the host, the principal guest asks the other guests if anyone would like more tea.

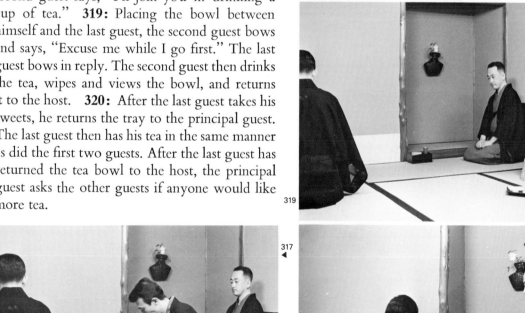

318

319

317
◄

320

321: If all decline, the host ladles hot water into the tea bowl and empties it into rinse-water container. 322: After he does this, the principal guest says to him, "We have had enough tea." The host replies, "Then allow me to finish now." 323: After the host has completed rinsing the utensils and added water to the kettle, and as he finishes placing the lid on the water container, the principal guest asks if he and the others may view the tea container and, if it is different from the one that was used for thick tea, the tea scoop. 324: These are set out, viewed, and returned, following the same procedures as were used during the serving of thick tea. The host then takes these utensils with him to the door of the preparation room and sets them near his knees. He bows to all the guests and then closes the door. The thin-tea part of the tea gathering is now finished.

322

323

321
◀

324

DEPARTURE

326

After taking these last utensils to the preparation room, the host opens the door again and comes partway into the tearoom. **325:** He then exchanges greetings with the guests. **326:** After this, the principal guest says to the host, "It is not necessary for you to see us out." **327:** The host then leaves the room, closing the door after him. **328:** The guests go in turn to view the flowers and the brazier. They then exit through the guest entrance; before he leaves, the last guest places the smoking utensils and tray for sweets near the host's door.

327

325
◄

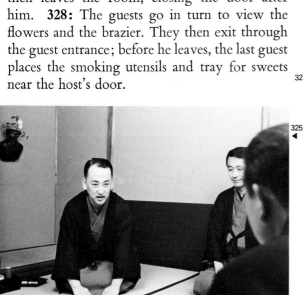

328

329: Once he is outside, the last guest closes the door of the guest entrance, making a slight noise as he does this. Hearing this sound, the host opens the door from the preparation room and removes the trays of smoking utensils and sweets. He then goes to the guest entrance and opens it to see the guests off. **330:** Hearing this, the guests turn toward the door, the principal guest having positioned himself so that he is the closest to the door. The guests bow to the host and then turn and leave. **331:** Looking out from the entrance, the host watches them until they are out of sight.

330

329
◄

►
331

6

PROCEDURES AND ETIQUETTE

BOWING AND STANDING

The Japanese people have long made the act of bowing an important part of social relationships. This is reflected in the large role it plays in the way of tea. A proper and graceful bow is an indication of a person's tea training. More important, it is a mirror of attitudes. A bow with the fingers apart and elbows in the air looks awkward to anyone. The amount of respect and humility in a person's heart is demonstrated by his bow. Because it is so important, the way of bowing should be the first thing learned by a student of tea. The attitude created by a bow can extend to all relationships. It is an example of how tea is a living part of our everyday lives.

SITTING BOW **1:** In order to bow correctly, one must first of all be sitting properly; the back should be straight and the shoulders relaxed; the right hand rests upon the left; the eyes are looking slightly downward. A graceful bow is made by tilting the body forward from the hips, keeping the back and head in a straight line. The hands should be in front of the knees, fingertips touching. There are three levels of formality in bowing: *shin, gyo,* and *so.* **2:** The shin bow, the most formal and polite, is used between the host and the guests. The deepest bow of the three, it is made with the hands flat on the floor. **3:** The semi-formal gyo bow, made with the fingers up to the second joint placed on the floor, is used between the guests. The body is not bent as far forward as in the formal bow. **4:** In the informal so bow, only the fingertips touch the floor. This is appropriate when the host is not in a position to make a more formal bow, or when short, informal remarks are exchanged between the guests.

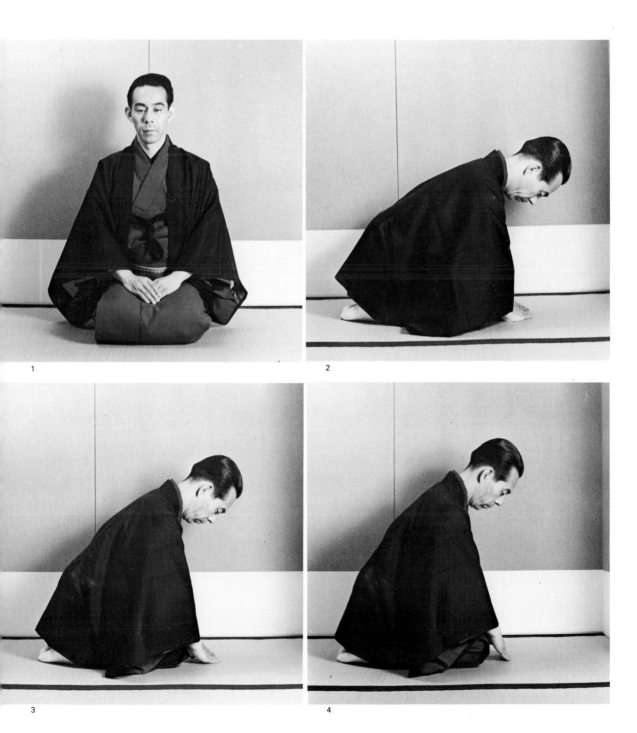

1

2

3

4

STANDING BOW   Although most bows at a tea gathering will be made from a sitting position, there are important times—such as when the host first greets the guests or when the guests take final leave of the host—when it is necessary to make a bow from a standing position. Just as in the sitting bow, one must be standing correctly in order to make a proper bow: the back should be straight and the shoulders relaxed; men should hold their hands at their sides, fingers together and slightly cupped so that the thumb and index finger touch; women's hands are positioned slightly higher and toward the front, fingers held together and the whole hand flattened on the thigh. Eyes should be cast slightly downward. Women should keep their feet together, while men spread theirs slightly. **5:** As with the sitting bow, there are three levels of formality for the standing bow: *shin, gyo,* and *so.* A formal shin bow is made by bending from the hips, keeping the back and head in a straight line. As the bow is made, the hands move to the knees; once they reach the knees, the bow is complete. This bow is used between the host and guests.   **6:** The semi-formal gyo bow is made in the same way, although the bow is now not so deep, the hands touching the leg approximately one-third up the thigh from the knee. This bow is used between guests.   **7:** The informal so bow, also used between guests, is made by tilting the body forward slightly and resting the hands on the upper part of the thigh.

STANDING UP   **8:** When sitting Japanese style, the feet are tucked under the body, the back is straight, and the hands rest lightly on the thighs. Preparing to stand up, one pauses momentarily, gathering strength and concentrating so that the movement will be carried out smoothly.   **9:** The toes are curled under the body, then the right knee raised and the right foot brought slightly forward.   **10:** The individual then stands straight up, keeping his back straight and allowing his arms to fall naturally to his sides.

5   6   7

8   9   10

OPENING AND CLOSING
SLIDING DOORS

1

It is important that the host correctly open and close the sliding doors between the preparation room and the tearoom. Depending upon the type of tearoom, the guests might also be called on to enter and exit through a sliding door rather than through a guest entrance. **1:** The fingers of the hand nearest the door pull are placed in the door pull and the door opened slightly. **2–3:** The fingers are slipped through the opening and placed on the edge of the door, about one foot above the floor, and the door is slid half-way open, so that the edge is directly in front of the center of the knees. **4–5:** The other hand, which has been resting on the thigh, is brought up, and the fingers are placed at the same height and used to push the door all the way open. **6–7:** When closing the door, the hand nearest it is used to pull the door halfway closed. **8:** The other hand, grasping the door at the same height, pulls it almost closed, leaving a slight opening. The thumb of the same hand is placed in the door pull, and the door is pushed closed completely.

5

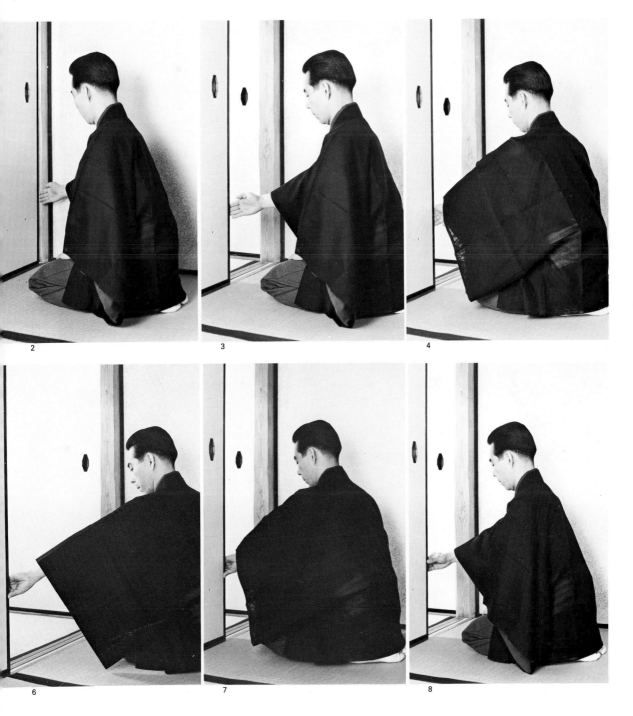

2

3

4

6

7

8

FOLDING A SILK WIPING CLOTH

1

The host folds the silk wiping cloth and tucks it in his obi before the guests arrive for the tea gathering. **1–2:** The host takes the silk wiping cloth, which has been folded into eighths, and places it on his left hand. **3:** He unfolds it once to the right. **4:** He takes the upper right-hand corner between his fingers. **5:** He then opens it all the way, thus naturally folding it into a triangle. **6–7:** He folds this triangle in half and takes it in his left hand. **8:** He tucks the upper corner of the cloth into his obi from the bottom. If a woman is hosting the tea gathering, she will tuck it into her obi from the top.

5

PURIFYING A CONTAINER
FOR THIN TEA

1

1: With his left hand the host grasps the silk wiping cloth, folds it under (women, who have their silk wiping cloths tucked in their obi from the top, fold them up), and removes it from his obi. **2:** Taking the far right corner of the triangle in his right hand, he unfolds the wiping cloth. **3:** The left-hand corner of the triangle is placed between the index finger and middle finger of his left hand and secured with the thumb. **4:** The right hand is then brought up and over, and with the left hand the hanging triangle is folded into thirds lengthwise, the cloth being held between the thumb and palm of the left hand. **5:** The palm of the left hand is turned up while the right hand folds the cloth down over the left thumb; the right index finger, moving along the top of the cloth, draws an imaginary line from left to right and the right hand folds the ends of the cloth under the left hand. **6:** The cloth is then transferred to the right hand and folded in half again with the left hand and secured in the right. **7:** The tea container is taken up with the left hand, and the far and near edges of the circular top are wiped. The cloth is then placed on top of the tea container, unfolded once, and used to wipe the top surface. **8:** Finished with the wiping, the host rests his right hand (still holding the folded cloth) on his thigh and sets the tea container down.

5

PURIFYING A TEA SCOOP

1: The folded silk wiping cloth is placed on the palm of the left hand and unfolded once, so that the two triangular ends are on the top. **2:** The uppermost end is taken up in the right hand and the cloth is folded in the same manner as for purifying a container for thin tea; however, after transferring it to the right hand, instead of folding it again with the left hand, it is placed on the left palm. **3:** The tea scoop is placed on top of the cloth. **4–5:** The wiping cloth is folded in half over the scoop; holding the end of the handle with the right thumb and index finger, the scoop is wiped up to the curved end. **6:** The cloth is brought back down to the middle of the scoop and is turned ninety degrees, and the sides wiped from the middle to the tip of the handle and then back again to the middle. **7:** Again turning the cloth, the upper and lower surfaces of the scoop are wiped from the middle to the curved end, then to the tip of the handle, and finally to the curved end again. **8:** Moving the cloth slightly beyond the curved end, the host rests his left hand (still holding the folded cloth) on his thigh and places the scoop in its proper position.

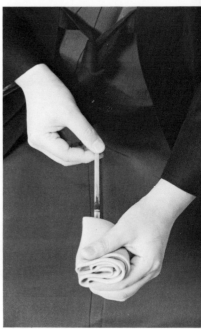

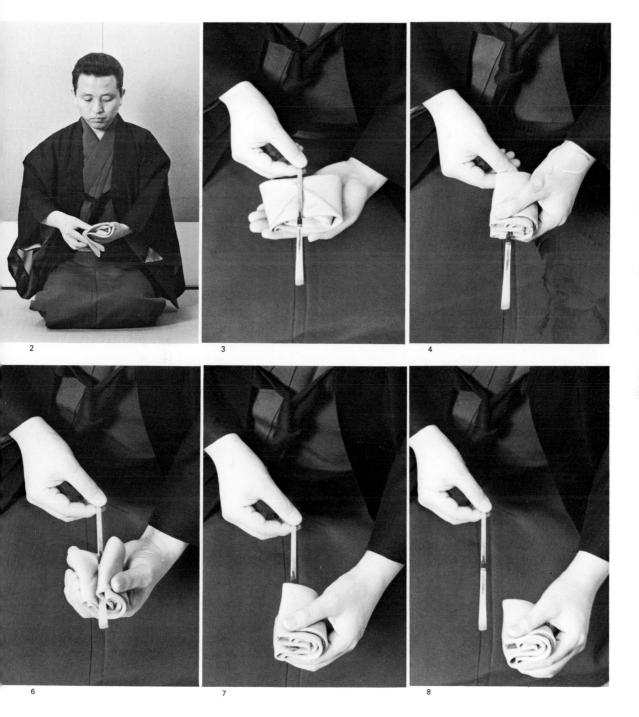

EXAMINING A TEA WHISK

1

1: With all the fingers placed on the tatami, the whisk is picked up with the thumb and index finger of the right hand. **2:** The whisk is set in the bowl, which is steadied by the left hand; the middle finger of the right hand rests on the edge of the bowl. **3:** The right hand is turned so that the thumb is on top, and the thumb and index finger grasp the whisk. **4:** The elbow is bent and the whisk lifted out of the bowl; the host examines the tines while the whisk is raised. **5:** While lowering the whisk, the host turns it about halfway toward himself and then replaces it in the bowl; steps 3, 4, and 5 are then repeated. **6:** Grasping it with the right thumb and index finger, the whisk is whisked a few times in the water. Next, starting at the far side of the edge of the water in the bowl, the whisk, still in the water, is brought around along the right side to the bottom of the circle, and then along the left, as if drawing a circle. **7:** The whisk is brought through the water to the center of the bowl and it is drawn up and toward the host while the finger tips of the left hand steady the bowl. **8:** As the left hand is placed on the thigh, the whisk is returned to its position, placing the fingers on the tatami while setting it down.

5

2

3

4

6

7

8

FOLDING A LINEN CLOTH

1–2: The linen cloth is first dampened and wrung dry. It is taken in both hands, opened fully lengthwise, and pulled taut to remove the wrinkles. **3–4:** Folding away from the host, the cloth is folded in one-third and then folded again. **5:** The right elbow is raised so that the cloth hangs lengthwise over the left knee; about halfway up, it is taken between the thumb and fingers of the left hand. **6:** As the palm of the left hand is turned up, the cloth is folded to the right over the left thumb; the right end is then folded under the left thumb. **7:** The right-hand fold is folded under slightly. **8:** The left thumb is removed, leaving a small opening running the width of the linen cloth.

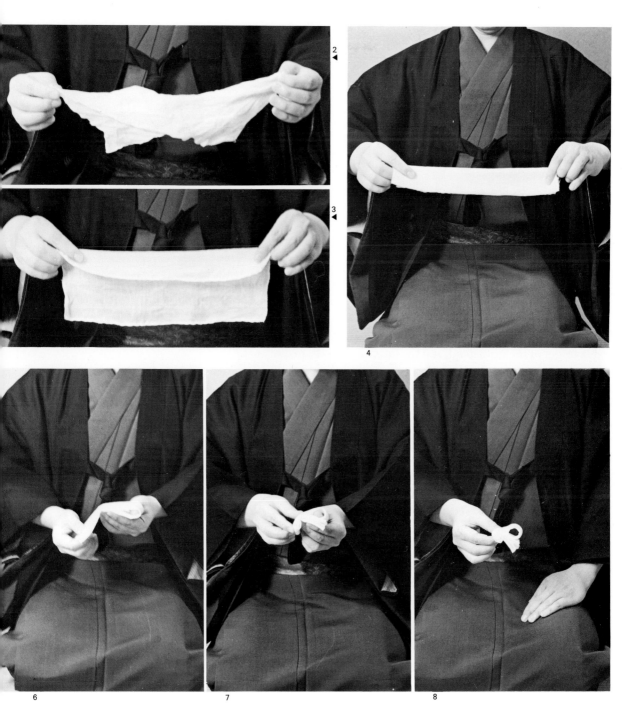

WIPING A TEA BOWL

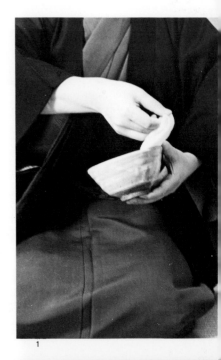

1: The folded linen cloth is placed in the bottom of the tea bowl so that the small opening running the width is toward the host, lying horizontally and parallel to him. With the bowl held in the left hand, the fold closest to the host is lifted out with the thumb and index finger of the right hand, and the linen cloth is draped over the left side of the rim. **2:** With the right thumb holding the cloth against the inner surface and the index finger holding it against the outer surface, the right hand brings the cloth toward the host and around the right side of the bowl until just before it comes to the thumb of the left hand. As the right hand grasps the tea bowl with the linen cloth, the left hand slightly releases its grip and the right hand turns· the tea bowl away from the host until it meets the thumb of the left hand. This movement is repeated four times, the last wipe ending at the far-right side of the bowl. **3:** The linen cloth is removed from the edge of the bowl. **4:** The cloth is placed in the bowl so that the side held by the four fingers is on the bottom. **5:** A small portion of the cloth is folded over from the top and then taken between the thumb and fingers. **6:** The left-hand inner surface of the bowl is wiped, then the right-hand. **7:** The inside bottom surface is wiped, the cloth drawing a short, out-ward-curving line on the left, and a similar line on the right. **8:** The cloth is placed in the bowl so that the side held by the four fingers is on the bottom, and the bowl is transferred from the left hand to the right hand and placed on the tatami.

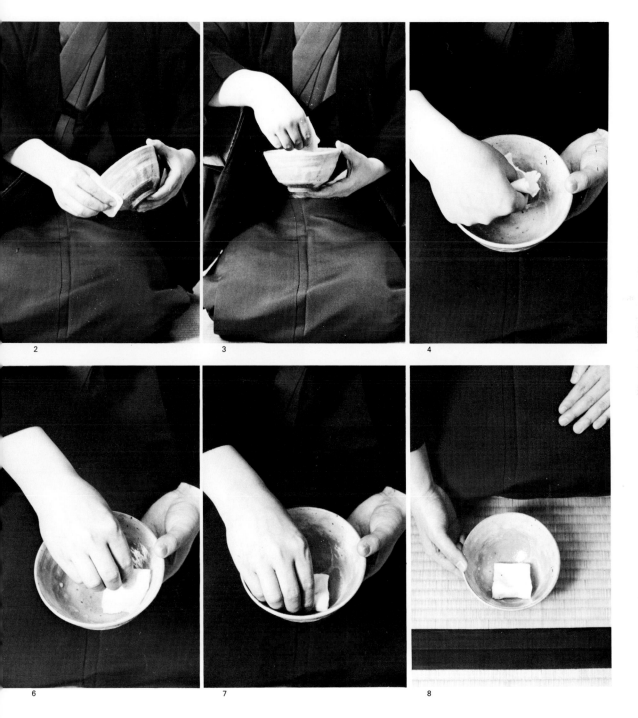

2

3

4

6

7

8

RESTING A WATER LADLE ON A KETTLE

OKI-BISHAKU MOVEMENT **1:** The scoop of the ladle is placed on the far edge of the kettle, the handle resting in the V between the thumb and index finger of the right hand. The handle is lightly held on the sides by the thumb and index finger, and the underside rests on the middle finger, which is bent in slightly. **2:** As the handle is set down, the thumb is brought over the handle and the index finger moves under the handle so that together they hold the handle near the joint in the bamboo. The handle is gently set down on the near edge of the kettle.

KIRI-BISHAKU MOVEMENT The ladle is held in the same position as in picture 1. **3:** The palm is opened and the thumb is straightened. **4:** The handle, resting on the thumb, is brought down and set on the edge of the kettle.

HIKI-BISHAKU MOVEMENT The ladle is held in the same position as in picture 1. **5:** Loosening its grip, the hand is slid slightly up the handle. **6:** The thumb is brought around just under the end of the handle and brought together with the other fingers so that the ladle rests on the middle finger. **7:** The fingers are slowly slid up to the end of the handle. **8:** As the ladle is lowered, the thumb is brought back to the end of the handle, the fingers bent, and the handle set on the near edge of the kettle.

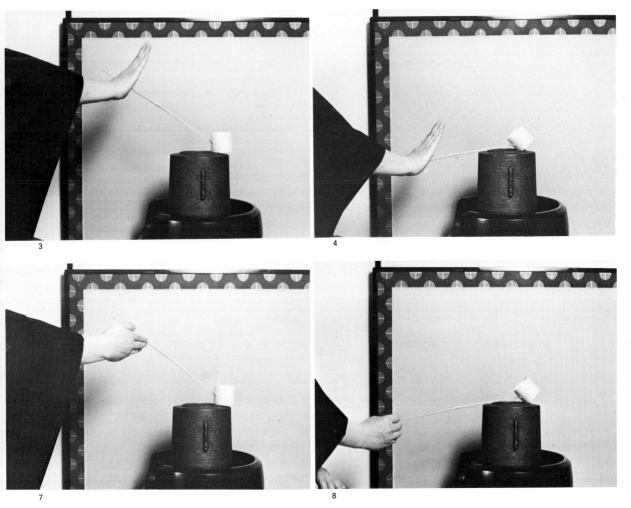

PARTAKING OF DRY SWEETS

1: The host places the plate of dried sweets in front of the principal guest. There are usually two types of dry sweets on the tray, one kind near the upper right-hand corner and one near the lower left-hand corner. As the host takes up the scoop to start making the thin tea, he bows and says to the principal guest, "Please have some sweets." After thanking the host, the guest leans forward to first admire the sweets. **2:** The principal guest bows to the second guest and says, "Excuse me while I go first." **3:** Picking up the plate and raising it slightly, the principal guest bows his head in appreciation. **4:** The principal guest takes the pad of white paper out from the breast of his kimono and places it in front of his knees. **5–6:** Using his fingers, the guest takes one or two of each kind of sweet, placing them on his pad of paper. **7:** Saying, "Please have some," the principal guest moves the plate of sweets toward the second guest. **8:** The principal guest takes up his pad of paper and begins to eat the sweets with his fingers.

1 ◄
2 ◄
3 ◄
4 ◄
5 ►
6 ►
7 ►
8 ►

PARTAKING OF MOIST SWEETS

After the host has placed a set of tiered, lacquered-wood boxes containing fresh, moist sweets in front of the principal guest, he returns to the door of the preparation room, sits, and bows, saying "Please have these sweets." All the guests bow in unison. The host then closes the door.   **1:** The principal guest then bows to the second guest, saying, "Excuse me while I go first." The principal guest lifts all the tiered boxes, bows his head in appreciation, and sets them down.   **2:** He then picks them up again except for the bottom one, and, turning them clockwise so that they are diagonal to the bottom box, he sets them down on top of it.   **3:** He takes up one of the wooden picks from the top of the set of boxes and places it in the lower right-hand corner of the bottom box, resting the pick on the rim of the box.   **4:** He then picks up all the boxes but the bottom one and places them to his left so that the second guest can reach them. At the same time, the second guest bows to the third guest, saying, "Excuse me while I go first."   **5:** The second guest then repeats the process of taking the bottom box. Meanwhile, the principal guest takes the folded pad of white paper from inside the breast of his kimono and places it on the tatami in front of his knees. Using the pick, he lifts the sweet out of the box and places it on the papers.   **6:** He then leans forward and, resting his elbows on his knees, picks up and examines the box.   **7:** This is repeated by each guest in turn. After each has taken his sweet and examined his box, all the boxes are passed down to the last guest, who restacks them and places them in front of the door to the preparation room.   **8:** The guests then take up the pads of paper and, using their picks, eat the sweets together.

PARTAKING OF THIN TEA

1: By the time the principal guest has finished eating his dry sweets, the host has prepared the bowl of thin tea for him and set it out. The guest moves forward, takes the bowl, and moves back to his place, setting the bowl in front of his knees. **2:** He takes the bowl up with his right hand and sets it down to his left. Bowing to the second guest, he says, "Excuse me while I go first." **3:** He then sets the bowl in front of his knees and, bowing, says to the host, "I will drink the tea." **4:** The principal guest picks up the bowl with his right hand and places it on the palm of his left. He raises the tea bowl with his right hand and bows his head in thanks. He then uses his right hand to turn the bowl 180 degrees clockwise, so that he will not drink from the "front." He raises the bowl to his lips and drinks the tea. **5:** When the guest finishes all the tea, he uses his thumb and index finger to wipe the rim of the bowl where his lips touched it. He then wipes his fingers on the pad of folded paper he carries in his kimono. He turns the bowl clockwise so that the "front" once again faces him. **6:** He then sets the bowl down. **7:** Leaning forward, the guest admires the general shape of the bowl. Next he picks it up with both hands and, resting his elbows on his knees, views it closely. After setting the bowl down again, he takes one last look at it, leaning forward with his hands on the tatami. He then picks up the bowl with his right hand and slides forward, setting the bowl on the tatami when he returns it to the host.

PARTAKING OF THICK TEA

The thick-tea part of the tea gathering differs from the thin-tea part in that with thick tea all the guests drink from the same bowl, passing it among themselves. When making thick tea, the host uses about eight times the amount of powdered tea and approximately one-third the amount of water used for thin tea. At the same time, the water is usually much hotter than that used to make thin tea. The guests will each wipe the rim of the bowl after drinking the thick tea; each should be carrying a slightly dampened and folded white linen cloth for this purpose. Since tea bowls other than those of the *Raku* type become rather hot to the touch when thick tea is made in them, the host, as in this example, should provide a piece of fabric *(kobukusa)* that the guests can use to hold the bowl. The manner of drinking thick tea is the same whether a portable brazier or a sunken hearth is utilized. The example presented here takes place in a room larger than four-and-a-half tatami mats, thus necessitating that the guests stand and walk at certain times; in a room of four-and-a-half mats or less, the guests slide on their knees.

1: After the thick tea is prepared, the host sets out the bowl, with the piece of fabric to the right.
2: The principal guest rises, standing on his right leg first, and goes forward to accept the bowl.
3–4: First sitting, he picks up the tea bowl with his right hand and places it on the palm of his left hand.   **5:** He then picks up the piece of fabric in his right hand, and, holding it against the side, he steadies the bowl.   **6:** Rising, he returns to his place, turning to his right before he sits down.

1

2 ◄

5 ▶

3 ◄

4 ◄

6 ▶

7: The principal guest puts the piece of fabric down to his right. **8:** Setting the bowl to his left, he bows, as do the guests, indicating that they will receive the tea together. **9:** The principal guest takes up the piece of fabric with his right hand and spreads it on the palm of his left. On top of this, he sets the tea bowl. Raising the bowl slightly, the principal guest bows his head in appreciation. Using his right hand, he then turns the bowl clockwise twice, or a total of 180 degrees, so that the "front" is facing away from him. **10:** Steadying the bowl with his right hand, the principal guest then takes one sip, making a slight slurping sound. **11:** The host then asks, "How is the tea?" The principal guest, placing his finger tips on the tatami, replies, "It is delicious." **12:** While the principal guest is taking his second sip, the second and the last guests bow to each other, the second guest saying, "Excuse me while I go first." The host turns toward the guests.

8

7

▶
9

The principal guest finishes drinking the tea, in this case taking about one-third of the quantity that is in the bowl, since there are three guests. Each guest usually takes three-and-a-half sips to drink his share. **13:** When the principal guest is finished, he puts the piece of fabric and tea bowl down in front of his knees, takes out his linen cloth, and wipes the rim of the bowl where his lips touched it.

14: Putting the linen cloth back in his kimono, he picks up the bowl and piece of fabric, places them on his left palm, and turns the bowl counterclockwise twice (180 degrees again) with his right hand so that the "front" is once more facing toward him. **15:** Turning slightly to his left, the principal guest hands the bowl and piece of fabric to the second guest. Both guests then face forward. **16:** As the second guest raises the bowl and slightly bows his head in appreciation, the principal guest bows, "sending off" the tea. After turning the bowl, the second guest then takes three-and-a-half sips of tea. As the second guest takes his first sip, the principal guest bows to the host, compliments him on the tea, and asks the names of the tea and its packer. After the host replies, the principal guest compliments him on the sweets, and the host bows. He then answers any other questions the principal guest might ask. After finishing his tea, the second guest wipes the rim of the bowl and turns the "front" of it toward himself. He then passes it to the next guest and bows. **17:** The next guest, in this example the last guest, receives and drinks the tea in the same manner as did the second guest. **18–20:** When he has finished, the last guest places the bowl in front of his knees, folds the piece of fabric in half, and puts it down to his left. As the last guest finishes drinking, the host turns and transfers a ladleful of water from the water container to the kettle.

14

15

16

17 ◀

18 ◀

19 ▶

20 ▶

21: At this point, the principal guest bows and asks the last guest, "May we examine the tea bowl?" The last guest bows in acknowledgment. **22:** The last guest uses his linen cloth to wipe the rim of the tea bowl where his lips touched it. **23–24:** Putting his linen cloth away, the last guest sets the tea bowl on his left palm, turns the bowl, picks up the piece of fabric in his right hand, and, holding it against the side, steadies the bowl.

21 ◄

23 ►

22 ◄

24 ►

25–26: The last guest stands, moves toward the principal guest, and sits. He puts the piece of fabric down, turns the tea bowl, and places the bowl and the piece of fabric in front of the principal guest. The last guest returns to his place. **27–28:** The principal guest picks up the piece of fabric in his right hand and puts it down to his right.

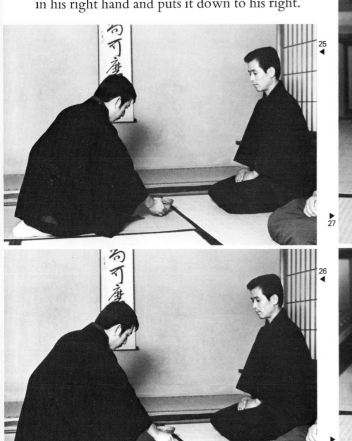

25
26
27
28

29: He bows to the second guest, saying, "Excuse me while I go first." The second guest bows in acknowledgment. **30:** With both hands on the floor in front of him, the principal guest leans forward to admire the general aspects of the tea bowl. **31:** Taking it up, he admires the shape, glaze, and feel of the bowl, as well as the remaining thick tea that clings to the inside; if the thick tea has been made correctly, there will be a glossy residue on the inside of a tea bowl. The guests appreciate this residue both for its own appearance and for the unique character it imparts to a tea bowl. As he holds the bowl in both hands, his elbows rest on his knees. Turning the bowl to admire it, he makes sure that one hand is always grasping the bowl firmly. While the principal guest views the tea bowl, the second guest bows to the next guest. After setting the bowl down again, he takes one more look at the bowl, leaning forward with his hands on the tatami. **32:** The principal guest then moves the bowl between himself and the second guest. **33:** While the second guest views the bowl, the principal guest admires the piece of fabric, noticing its weave, texture, coloring, and so on.

30

29
◄

►
31

34: The second and the last guests then view the bowl and the piece of fabric. **35–36:** When the last guest has finished, he puts the two items to his left.

37: The last guest, carrying the bowl and piece of cloth, and the principal guest both move forward and sit adjacent to the host; the last guest puts the bowl and piece of cloth in front his knees and then places each in front of the principal guest. The last guest returns to his place.   **38:** The principal guest places the bowl, its "front" facing toward the host, and the piece of fabric in the same location as they were originally placed by the host.   **39:** The host takes the piece of fabric and places it inside his kimono, picks up the bowl, and, after turning slightly, places it in front of his knees. The host and guests bow in unison.

37
◄

▶
38

39

GLOSSARY-INDEX

metal rings *(kan),* 20
mizusashi, see water container
mizuya, see preparation room
moist sweets *(namagashi),* 47–51; partaking of, 110, 168–69
morning tea gathering *(asa chaji),* 62
movements at tea gathering, 4
Murata Shuko (1422–1502), tea master, 6
Mushanokoji-Senke school of tea, 7
Myoe (1173–1232), Buddhist priest and exponent of tea, 5

nakadachi, see intermission
namagashi, see moist sweets
nijiriguchi, see guest entrance
Noami (1397–1471), tea master, 5
Nobunaga, *see* Oda Nobunaga
November tea gathering, see *kairo*

Oda Nobunaga (1534–81), military dictator and tea aficionado, 6
Okakura Tenshin (Kakuzo), tea authority and author of *The Book of Tea,* 8
oki-bishaku movement for resting water ladle on kettle, 164
Omote-Senke school of tea, 7
opening and closing sliding doors, 150–51
Oribe, *see* Furuta Oribe
oyose (tea gathering with many guests), 62

partaking of dry sweets, 166–67
partaking of moist sweets, 168–69
partaking of thick tea, 172–82
partaking of thin tea, 170–71
pick, see *kuromoji*
plan of tea structures and garden, 18
portable brazier *(furo),* 22
pottery, *see* ceramics
powdered tea, viii, 46
preparation room *(mizuya),* 17
preparations for tea gathering: by guests, 62–63; by host, 3–4, 56; *see also* utensils and decorations
preparing the silk wiping cloth, 152–53
Preservation of Health Through Drinking Tea, see *Kissa Yojoki*
procedures and etiquette, 145–82
purifying a container for thin tea, 154–55
purifying a tea scoop, 156–57

Raku chawan (Raku tea bowls), 34

Raku tea bowls, see *Raku chawan*
reception-room tea gathering, see *shoin cha*
refreshments, 45–60
resting water ladle on kettle, 164–65
returning to tearoom after intermission, 114–17
Rikyu (Sen Rikyu; 1522–91), tea master, 2–3, 6, 7, 34
rinse-water container *(kensui),* 24
ritual purification, 10, 68, 70–71
ro, see sunken hearth
robuchi (wooden frame for sunken hearth), 22
roji, see garden

sadoguchi (host's entrance), 76
sakè as item of *kaiseki* cuisine, 56
second arranging of charcoal, 130–35
sekimori-ishi (guard stones), 70
Sekishu, *see* Katagiri Sekishu
Sekishu school of tea, 7, 8
sencha (medium-quality green tea), viii
Senke schools of tea, 7, 8
Sen Rikyu, *see* Rikyu
Sen Sotan (1578–1658), tea master, 7
Seven Enshu Kilns, 7
sheltered waiting arbor *(koshikake machiai),* 10, 14
shifuku, see bag for thick-tea container
shin bow, 146–47, 148–49
shoburo (May tea gathering), 22
shoin cha (reception-room tea gathering), 5
Shotoku (572–622), prince and regent, 5
Shuko, *see* Murata Shuko
silk wiping cloth *(fukusa),* 63; preparation of, 152–53
sitting bow, 146–47
sliding doors, opening and closing of, 150–51
smoking utensils, 65, 136
Soami (1472–1523), tea master, 5
soan cha (grass-hut tea), 6
so bow, 146–47, 148–49
Sochin, tea master, 6
Sotan, *see* Sen Sotan
sound of simmering water, see *matsukaze*
split-toed socks, see *tabi*
standing bow, 148–49
standing up, 148–49
stone water basin *(tsukubai),* 10, 14
structures and garden, 10–18

The "weathermark" identifies this book as a production of Weatherhill, Inc., publishers of fine books on Asia and the Pacific. Supervising editor: James T. Conte. Book design and typography: Meredith Weatherby and Yoshihiro Murata. Layout of illustrations: Yoshihiro Murata. Production superivsor: Yutaka Shimoji. Composition: Samhwa, Seoul. Printing and binding: Oceanic Graphics Printing Company, Hong Kong.